Teaching the Way Students Learn

*Practical Applications
for Today's Classrooms*

Edited by Jill E. Cole

ROWMAN & LITTLEFIELD EDUCATION
A division of
ROWMAN & LITTLEFIELD PUBLISHERS, INC.
Lanham • New York • Toronto • Plymouth, UK

Published by Rowman & Littlefield Education
A division of Rowman & Littlefield Publishers, Inc.
A wholly owned subsidiary of The Rowman & Littlefield Publishing Group, Inc.
4501 Forbes Boulevard, Suite 200, Lanham, Maryland 20706
www.rowman.com

10 Thornbury Road, Plymouth PL6 7PP, United Kingdom

British Library Cataloguing in Publication Information Available

Library of Congress Cataloging-in-Publication Data

Library of Congress Cataloging-in-Publication Data Available
ISBN 978-1-61048-056-7 (cloth : alk. paper)—ISBN 978-1-61048-057-4 (pbk. : alk. paper)—ISBN
978-1-61048-058-1 (electronic)

™ The paper used in this publication meets the minimum requirements of American
National Standard for Information Sciences Permanence of Paper for Printed Library
Materials, ANSI/NISO Z39.48-1992.

Printed in the United States of America

This book is dedicated to my husband, Tom, without whose love, support, and assistance this book would not have been completed.

Contents

Prologue

Once upon a time there was a classroom, one of thousands in the United States where students expect to learn and a teacher wants to teach. But this classroom is special. It is your classroom. It is a "one of a kind" classroom—because of you, the teacher.

Your students may represent a diversity of cultures, races, abilities, struggles, talents, and personalities. Your classroom is, no doubt, a busy place that is sometimes messy, sometimes chaotic, and hopefully alive with passion and laughter and learning. You are persevering in the confusing atmosphere of today's educational environment, but you still ask—am I reaching my students? Are they really learning?

It is the purpose of this book to offer practical ideas to help your students learn.

In this book you will find a rich compilation of instructional strategies from experienced educators and administrators that reflect their own "one of a kind" classroom experiences. The power of the strategies presented in this book emanate from the contributors' practice of a constructivist philosophy of learning and teaching. They have found that this philosophy explains how we, as human beings, learn the way we do and how we can support learning in our students.

As you read the authors' chapters, you will see philosophy taken into practice. One of the goals of this book is to make the constructivist paradigm doable in the classroom. You will also read our Teaching Memoirs that illustrate our personal experiences with constructivist teaching and students. Everything does not always proceed smoothly, but the struggle is worth it. Teachers make a difference in students' lives!

The chapters and memoirs will reveal diversity in voice and tone. We will demonstrate how we put constructivism into practice in distinctive ways. We hope that you sense the excitement and dedication in the voices that are included in this volume.

Jamie, Marcia, and Jill are teacher educators who want to support and encourage teachers. They provide the paradigm as well as the practical ideas that can promote change in the classroom. Laura, Charmaine, Kathy, and Patti are classroom teachers who provide strategies straight from their own classrooms. And all the memoir authors augment the paradigm and strategies with personal experiences.

Teaching and learning is a process, of course, with goals that go beyond a single academic year. Teaching is a career-long endeavor that might be best illustrated by a continuum: never-ending and always changing. Encouraging and supporting each other along the way is a privilege as well as a responsibility. Here is our story. Join us on the journey . . .

Acknowledgments

First, I would like to thank all the contributing authors for sharing their content expertise and their passion for teaching. Everyone was so generous with their time: sharing stories, discussing chapters, writing drafts, revising, and preparing the final manuscript. It was a journey I was privileged to share with these colleagues and friends.

Thanks also go to those who took the time and energy to read and give feedback on the manuscript. Diana Williamson, Jane Ragains, Allen Zipke, Doug Grudzina, and Dr. Steven Layne were honest and informative. Their comments made such a difference in the finished book.

Finally, I want to express my appreciation to Dr. Tom Koerner, vice president and editorial director, for his support and encouragement during this process. He and Lindsey Schauer, assistant editor, were always quick to respond to my many emailed questions. Thank you.

Chapter One

The Constructivist Paradigm: Teaching the Way Students Learn

Jill E. Cole

Often, educators call constructivism a theory or an approach, but the authors of this book prefer philosophical paradigm. A philosophy is "a system of values by which one lives" (American Heritage College Dictionary, 2004, p. 1045) and a paradigm is a "pattern or model" (American Heritage College Dictionary, 2004, p. 1008) for those values, concepts, and practices. It is not enough to merely "do" constructivism; in fact it might be impossible. An educator must "be" a constructivist, using the philosophy to guide teaching.

A teacher, a school, a parent, even a student must believe that constructivism is the best way to learn for it to become most effective. And when they experience its results and "buy in" to the philosophy, they will never teach, or learn, the same again.

Constructivism is a philosophy of how we learn (and not about how we teach). It posits that human beings learn by constructing new knowledge through connections to current knowledge and experiences. Learning, then, is a process of adjusting existing understandings to accommodate new experiences. Teaching the way students learn is not simply disseminating content but is a carefully structured series of learner events that uncover students' existing understandings and use them to present new information.

This is in opposition to the notion that children are empty vessels waiting to "be filled" by their teachers. Constructivist educators strive to teach not only to the content standards but also to the child's needs and interests. Constructivism originally emerged from learning theory *and* classroom-based research, making it a valid model for teachers and students in real classrooms.

In short, constructivists believe the following about the classroom experience (Brooks & Brooks, 2001):

- Learners need developmentally appropriate instruction so they can construct their own knowledge. Their opinions and questions are valued and integral to the process. For example, constructivist teachers actively form positive relationships with their students by asking about their interests and previous experiences, encouraging their questions, and involving them in setting the rules and structure of the classroom.
- Teachers facilitate meaning construction by seeking students' current perceptions before planning appropriate lessons. For example, they pose important questions, encourage conversation, and allow risk-taking in learning without penalty. They help students connect the new learning to their real lives.
- The curriculum includes multiple resources, such as primary sources and manipulatives, and is presented from whole to part with emphasis on big concepts. For example, the classroom contains a variety of fiction and nonfiction beyond textbooks, and students are encouraged to explore themes like "conflict" and "cause and effect" as they read.
- Teachers and students set collaborative goals for learning as well as behaviors in the classroom. For example, teachers and students together may set learning goals for a cross-curricular unit on "culture in America" as well as for the structure and governance of small group discussions that will take place during the unit.
- Assessment of student work (formative and summative) is interwoven with teaching. For example, teachers look at student work formatively to see what the students don't know yet so future instruction can be planned, and then summatively, once the teacher feels all students' instructional needs have been met and they are ready to present their new knowledge.

This book describes constructivist teaching that can be used in any school to engage students and achieve learning. Those of us working in schools are a diverse group of people. We are teachers and parents, administrators and coaches, students and teacher educators. But what holds this unique group together is a genuine effort to seek out important content, effective strategies, and relationships that inspire student learning.

Constructivism lies on a continuum. We will never arrive at the end and be "perfect constructivists." But we can move toward better constructivist teaching a little each day, discovering unsuspected truths along the way, traveling alternate pathways at times, or even stopping to take a rest.

The continuum is a lifelong undertaking that sometimes feels like taking one step forward and two steps back. But when we look at our progress over time, we see that movement has occurred, lessons have been learned, and challenges have been overcome. This is the epitome of teachers and students learning and growing together, and any educator, any school can choose to teach this way—the way students learn.

REFERENCES

American Heritage College Dictionary (2004). (4th ed.). Boston: Houghton Mifflin.

Brooks, J. G., & Brooks M. G. (2001). *The case for constructivist classrooms*. Upper Saddle River, NJ: Prentice-Hall.

Teaching Memoir: Constructivist Teaching 101

D. Colette Wheatley

One summer a group of fifth-grade teachers from my school took a course in which we developed a constructivist science unit called "Heat and Temperature." The constructivist paradigm was new to us. Normally we taught from a traditional textbook instituted by the district. With this new "approach," we were acting as facilitators while giving our students lots of opportunities to construct their own understanding through carefully planned, inquiry-based learning activities. This required a lot more work from the teachers to create meaningful lessons to help students develop their understanding of the intended concepts.

We began by asking our students to make predictions about what they thought the outcome of the particular experiment would be. My classroom was composed of a variety of academic levels as it was an inclusion classroom. Many of my students, regardless of their academic level, struggled with the concept of making predictions. It was something that they did not usually do in a traditional science lesson. They were used to teachers giving them the information to learn instead of asking them to think on their own about what would happen and *why*!

After the students made their predictions, we conducted our experiment. The students were asked to revisit their predictions and reflect on (although we didn't use the term reflect at that time) why the outcome occurred as it did.

My "aha" moment about the effectiveness of constructivism occurred when one of my special education students spoke up while observing the experiment, "Can I change my prediction?" The outcome of the experiment was still unclear, but she was able to "see ahead" to what was going to happen! This child often was unable to grasp science information that was presented by her teacher, but when she actually *experienced the science* she was able to construct meaning for herself.

This small classroom event was a major turning point for this particular student and for me as a constructivist teacher. Upon reflecting about what had happened in my classroom, I realized that this was *the* way to help my students construct meaningful understandings in science, and later also in math. Instead of a dispenser of facts, I became a facilitator of knowledge through the use of thematic units, meaningful concepts, and activities in which my students were actively involved in their own learning.

Chapter Two

The 20 Percent Solution: An Early Literacy Framework for Struggling Readers

Marcia P. Lawton

Ask any experienced first-grade teacher how many of her children are not reading fluently by the end of first grade, and teachers will tell you four or five children. In most classrooms that is about 20 percent of the children.

This number is surprisingly consistent from classroom to classroom, from year to year, and through all of the various "reforms" that have been presented as the latest, greatest solution to the "reading" problem. By the end of the first-grade year, according to an informal poll of teachers, about 80 percent of children are decoding relatively fluently; 20 percent are not. (Clay's [1993] work supports this idea. Her Reading Recovery model targets the bottom 20 percent of first graders.)

This 80/20 split also shows up in research on various methods for teaching early literacy skills. When researchers evaluate the effectiveness of various programs or methods, the results generally show that approximately 80 percent of children learn to read using whatever method is being tested; 20 percent will not.

If about 80 percent of children learn to read without difficulty, perhaps learning to read is generally not the very difficult task that is implied by the "literacy crisis" policy makers. Many children come to school with the basics of literacy knowledge already in place. Others learn quickly and easily.

As easily and naturally as most children learn to decode printed symbols, however, there are the 20 percent who find the task more daunting. The fate of the 20 percent has been a concern for many years. Much of the current testing movement, and the prescriptive teaching materials that have grown out of the testing movement, owe their existence to concern about early literacy learning for the 20 percent.

This chapter presents an Early Literacy Framework, a social constructivist framework for working with all young children, but especially children who take longer to learn the decoding and encoding processes. This framework addresses underlying concepts and principles often overlooked in early literacy instruction while maintaining a strong emphasis on comprehension and critical thinking about text from the beginning of literacy instruction.

The Early Literacy Framework addresses two knowledge components:

• knowledge of the purposes of written language
• knowledge of the nature of written language

Each of these knowledge components will be addressed separately and will include the following:

• description of the content to be learned
• activities for helping children develop the knowledge
• assessment strategies to help teachers evaluate children's knowledge

Before looking at each of the knowledge components, it is important to look at the history of early literacy research from which these two bodies of knowledge have grown. Current understanding of early literacy learning has been influenced by many years of literacy research, research which began under a behaviorist paradigm, and was developed and significantly redirected under a constructivist paradigm. One concern is that, presently, the advances made under constructivist and social/constructivist research paradigms are being lost.

RESEARCH IN A BEHAVIORIST PARADIGM

Prior to the 1970s, most research was conducted using a behaviorist paradigm. Studies on early reading were based on task analyses of the reading process. Experts—adults who already knew how to read—broke the reading/ writing processes into individual bits of knowledge. This list (a task analysis) was referred to as "skills" and included such things as

• letter names,
• letter sounds (broken down into hundreds of pieces such as consonants, short vowels, blends, digraphs, long vowels, etc.),

- sight words,
- sentence reading,
- paragraph reading,
- story reading, and
- various ideas related to comprehension—sequencing, determining main idea, inferring, generalizing, synthesizing.

Breaking down literacy tasks into component parts was an important part of the research on how our written language system works. However, *this research presented the thinking of literate adults looking back on the task rather than a study of how children view the tasks.* These bits of knowledge that began as a way to study the features of our written language system rather quickly generated into a teaching method.

The "bits and pieces" research coincided with the era of Henry Ford and the assembly line. Automobile assembly lines were based on a task analysis for the construction of cars—build a chassis, attach a drive train, and so on. It was easy to do the same thing for children in schools. In kindergarten, teach letter names. In first grade, teach sounds. This method makes perfect sense from the point of view of the skilled adult who is being influenced by behaviorist theories and assembly-line methods and is also looking back on dimly remembered early literacy instruction.

The bits of knowledge were usually considered to be hierarchical. Children were expected to learn the smallest bits first—thus the learning of the alphabet is a first step in learning to read in almost every school in the country, even though naming letters is probably one of the most abstract tasks we ask children to do.

Research prior to the 1970s was generally about developing methods for teaching these "skills" and assessing the results of the instruction. Research questions tended to be of the type: Do children learn better with direct instruction or with a basal system? Which basal system is the most effective? What reward systems will be most motivating for children? In what order should the letter/sound combinations be taught?

RESEARCH IN AN EMERGENT LITERACY PARADIGM

Beginning in the late 1960s and early 1970s, a different paradigm began to set a new agenda for early literacy research. The work of Downing (1970), Sawyer (1992), Sulzby (1985), Meltzer and Herse (1969), Reid (1966), and many others came to be called "emergent literacy" and was a *completely different way of viewing how children learn to read.* The use of the word "emergent" to describe this research emphasizes the developmental and often haphazard way in which children learn important concepts and principles.

THEORY BOX: PIAGET

Piaget gave us three very important ideas (actually probably lots more than that):

1. Children do not think like adults.
2. We can study children's thinking by watching them perform tasks and asking them questions about their thinking.
3. Children will gradually develop understanding of important concepts in somewhat predictable stages.

In the emergent literacy era, researchers used qualitative methods to focus on children and their natural learning. Piaget's (1995) theories were well-known. From Piaget, researchers learned the value of carefully designed and documented case studies of individual children.

Piaget's research showed us that children do not think like adults and really are not capable of thinking like adults. Instead of trying to measure children's ability to match adult thinking, emergent literacy researchers tried *to understand the unique ways in which children think about literacy tasks.* The research questions in literacy changed from "What is the best method for teaching children to read?" to "How do children understand the literacy process? What are they thinking as they interact with print?"

Emergent literacy researchers did case studies on individual children—at first, often their own children. Following the lead of Piaget, these researchers kept field notes as they watched children interacting with print and asked them to explain their thinking. The earliest studies followed children who learned to read without formal instruction, usually before they entered school.

Many, many similar studies were conducted in the 1970s and 1980s and themes emerged. It soon became clear that there are concepts and principles related to decoding our written symbols that often caused confusion for children. Teachers had always known that some children learned to read almost by magic, effortlessly and pleasurably, while others seemed to languish, not able to progress. The research of emergent literacy helped to explain those difficulties.

THEORY BOX: CHILDREN'S THINKING

Piaget showed in his research that children at different ages had very different ideas about what was important.

In his liquid volume experiment, children watched as water was poured into two identical glasses. The level of the water in both glasses was the same.

When the liquid from one was poured into a different glass with a different shape—taller and thinner or wider and shorter—children younger than seven or eight believed that the amount of water had changed. When the water was returned to the original glasses, those children believed that the amount of water was again the same.

Children younger than seven or eight did not know the relevant features of the task. The focus was on the appearance of the water, not on the quantity. They did not view the task as adults might.

While it is true that children also learn factual information, such as names and sounds of letters, the new research demonstrated that the factual information was not sufficient for learning to read and, in fact, sometimes got in the way. Children need to know the *relevant features* of print—concepts and principles that define our written language system. They need to consider these questions: What is important to look at and study? What can be safely ignored?

So, what are the relevant features of print identified in emergent literacy research that children might not immediately notice? These features can be divided into the two knowledge components of the Early Literacy Framework:

- Features related to the *purpose of written language*
- Features related to the *nature of written language*

For adults these concepts were learned long ago and are no longer considered in any conscious way; adults do not think about them as they read. For young children just beginning to understand how print works, these concepts are not obvious. Teachers of young children must understand the importance of this knowledge and be aware that such knowledge is not obvious to the novice.

PURPOSE OF WRITTEN LANGUAGE

Why do we read and write? Of what value is this activity? Adults know that reading and writing are tools that can help us communicate, provide memory support, entertain us, help us learn new information, and so on. These purposes may not be readily apparent to young children.

Children learn the use of common everyday tools by observing others use them and attempting to use them, too. Many examples come to mind: using a spoon, drinking from a glass, using a remote to control the TV, opening a door, hitting something with a hammer, turning on the faucet for the outside hose, squirting people. This learning is effortless because its value is always apparent, the purpose is clear—and perhaps determined by the child.

Three-year-old Kole loved to squirt people with the hose. When his dad turned the faucet off to keep him from squirting, he quickly learned how to turn it back on. He had a clear purpose in mind, observed his dad, and imitated the *relevant* behavior to achieve his purpose.

Written language is also a tool (Vygotsky 1962). Most children who see adults using written language in their home—just as they are exposed to and learn the value of food preparation, care of the home and clothing, and other common adult activities—will gradually learn the purpose and value of written language.

Not all children have access to books in their homes, but almost all children see literate activity of some sort. As with any tool, however, simple exposure to literacy will not be enough for all children to learn the *relevant features* related to the purpose of written language. Children must "notice" what adults are doing with print and why.

A child who observes someone hammering will pick up a hammer and swing it. There are refinements that they will not be aware of immediately— relevant features of hammering yet to learn. Which part of the handle do you hold? How far back does the swing start? Which part of the head is the business end? Aiming is necessary. How does one do that? What should the hammerer be aiming at? What is the goal of the task?

When he turned four, Kole began attending a preschool two mornings a week. He often plays "restaurant" with his grandmother, who has a kitchen play set in her house. Kole knows that servers in restaurants write notes about the customers' orders. His parents take him places and study the menu with him to decide what he wants to eat. When he plays restaurant, he gets a pad of paper and a pencil and "writes" little marks, a different set of marks for each item ordered. He is learning about the purpose of written language.

As Kole gets older, he will gradually develop a more sophisticated understanding of written language *purposes* and will learn more about the *nature* of written language. This learning will be natural and pleasant because it is contextual and sensible to his four-year-old thinking. Kole's preschool teacher wants him to learn the alphabet. So far, he is not really interested. Kole's lack of interest in learning the alphabet points out the importance of understanding purpose. Purpose often provides motivation for learning the task.

Activities to Learn Purpose of Written Language

Read to Children

One of the best ways to help children notice these purposes is to *read to them*—all kinds of reading: story books, newspapers, magazines, mail, computer screens, reference books, food labels, and so on. Especially in kindergarten and first grade, teachers should read three or four times a day for different purposes and discuss the texts. "Let's look in this book to find out how to feed our turtle." "Where is Iraq? Johnny's mother is there." "Did everyone sign up for lunch? Let's read the menu."

Model the Use of Text and Call Attention to the Purposes

If adults call attention to the many uses of print, the children will begin to notice these features on their own. Parents who point to a menu and ask children what they want to eat and then read the menu will be modeling the purposes of print.

All teachers need to read to their students. This is one of those research findings that is so well known as to be a truism. But, in addition to reading, teachers need to take the opportunity to point out issues related to the purpose of using text. This is important for all children, but especially for those who have not "noticed" print yet.

Model the Use of Writing in Everyday Tasks

In like manner, if adults *model the uses of writing*, children will develop an appreciation for writing—reminders on the refrigerator, grocery lists, notes to friends, family stories, checks, calendar entries, funny jokes someone told, greeting cards, email messages, and so on. This modeling needs to be "noticed" by the children in order for them to gradually learn these purposes. Adults need to explicitly point out the uses of print.

In a second-grade classroom, three children are talking about their trip to the state park. They have collected some leaf samples and are attempting to identify them. Sam and Alexis decide to go find reference books. Madison begins a search online. Using both the books and the Internet, the children try to find matching samples. They find conflicting information. Alexis and Madison decide to write a list of the possibilities and ask the teacher later.

The children in this example have an understanding of the purpose of written language. They are using text and their own writing to help accomplish a task. It should be noted, however, that they might need some help on the relevant features of leaf identification.

If children understand why they are learning something, they are more likely to apply themselves to learning and sustain the effort through confusions. Understanding how written language is used and why can provide an important context that makes the task of learning to read and write a sensible process instead of just another ambiguous thing that happens in school.

Create Charts of Different Types and Purposes of Print

One way that teachers can help children connect home activities with school is to bring the children's home discourses into the school. Almost everyone has literacy activities of some type at home. They may not read books or practice writing letters, but most children have seen some literacy activity. It might be using the TV guide channel on television, reading text on a computer, reading signs on the street to find an office you need to visit, filling out forms, giving your order to a waiter, who writes it down, and so on.

After a discussion of the multiple types and purpose of print materials, teachers might assign children to bring in things (or just tell something) that people in their family read. As children and teacher discuss the texts, children will begin to find multiple personal reasons for reading and writing. Making a home connection could help children notice literate activity in their homes or in family activities. An assignment like this from school could help parents understand the importance of modeling these activities for their children.

Make charts of these types of print to hang in the classroom. For example, Sara, who speaks Spanish as a first language, brought in a grocery list her mother had made. Ask Sara to share the list, tell what her mother wrote, and then create a chart to document the event.

Sara's mother wrote a list of the things she needed at the store.
Sara's mother writes in Spanish.
Here is what she needed:

   pescado (fish)
   cereales (cereal)

fideo (pasta)

Children can use charts like this as early literacy practice. Review charts each day for several days after they are created. Some teachers create charts for all kinds of purposes related to classroom work—lists of rules for feeding the hamster, lists of who has what job this week, daily schedules, reminders of special events or holidays. When the charts are no longer current, they can be removed from the wall and bound with others into a book that children can choose to read during free reading time. These texts will be personally important to the children who helped create them.

Infuse Dramatic Play Centers with Purposeful Literate Activities

For many years, kindergarten classrooms included dramatic play centers where children could dress up and pretend to be adults in real-life settings. Typically, the play centers had kitchens with recipe books, grocery lists on the refrigerator, calendars to be filled in, and so on. Many teachers changed these centers periodically to provide other contexts, such as restaurants, doctors or veterinarian offices, grocery or other types of stores. Unfortunately, this very valuable practice has disappeared from many early childhood classrooms under pressure from high-stakes testing. Many teachers also report not having enough time to read to, and with, children.

Rather than curtailing this activity, the use of play centers should be a standard activity for preschool, kindergarten, and into first grade. Our current short-sighted focus on drill and practice has created confusion for many children who have not learned the purpose of written language.

For children who have learned literacy purposes outside of school, this oversight might not be so important, although critical motivation to learn may be missing for many. However, for our 20 percent, this oversight could be critical to their later learning. In the current drill and practice climate, if a child does not learn the prescribed bits and pieces, the child must continue to work on them and will not have the opportunity to move on to the interaction with print that would help to provide context and purpose to the learning of letter names and other factual knowledge. The context and purpose need to be part of all literacy activity.

Help Children Adopt a "Meaning-Making Stance" toward Written Text

Activities focused on the purpose of print have another outcome. When children are asked to focus on purpose, they are naturally developing a *meaning-making stance*. Reading and writing are meaning-making activities.

Teachers of older children notice that many students lack the ability to comprehend text. "He can read, but he has comprehension problems" is a common observation. Perhaps the source of some of the problem is the lack of a meaning-making stance in early literacy activities. When children experience only drill and practice methods or mindless reading of fractured text, they are learning that the purpose of print is to get the words right, or to read all the words as fast as you can, or to answer the questions on a computer quiz. Literacy skills should not be addressed for any length of time outside of a meaning-making stance.

Two young men in high school have been identified as having reading "problems." When asked to read an IRI (Informal Reading Inventory) passage, Kyle misreads several words. If the miscue makes sense, he continues to read. If it does not make sense, he returns and tries to work out the problem word. If he cannot work it out, he will continue reading. Sometimes something in the text cues him to go back and figure out the earlier miscue. Kyle understands reading for purpose. When asked questions about the text, he is able to answer most of them. Kyle has a meaning-making stance. He knows that the text should have meaning and actively tries to work out the meaning.

Erik reads very quickly. There are many miscues, but Erik just keeps on reading. Sometimes the words he reads are not real words. When asked about the passage, Erik has no idea what it was about. Erik is not reading for a purpose and does not have a meaning-making stance.

These two young men have very different reading issues and need very different interventions. Kyle's reading will improve when he finds text that he enjoys reading—thus increasing the amount of time he spends reading. His current strategies will work well for him with more practice. He will increase his sight vocabulary as he spends more time reading.

Erik needs to find purpose for reading, probably through discussion with others about a text of mutual interest. Until he has a meaning-making stance, other instruction will not lead to improvements. Placing him in a phonics drill and practice program—currently a common treatment for almost any literacy issue—will only exacerbate the problem.

Assessing Children's Knowledge of Purpose of Print

Teachers in kindergarten and first grade will have children with many different experiences with print. It is critical for the 20 percent, especially, that teachers are sensitive to children's understanding of the uses and value of print and take opportunities to observe and assess this knowledge.

ASSESSMENT STRATEGIES

1. Observe children at work and play and keep field notes.
2. Ask children about their use of written language in a particular situation.
3. Use the Purpose of Written Language Inventory, appendix A.

Teachers must give children opportunities to use print-related activities in natural settings, observe their use of the materials (for example, Kole writing food orders or the second graders working on leaves), and talk to children about what they are doing. In other words, one of the best ways to assess this knowledge is in a Piagetian-type observation and interview. This is particularly important with young children and with those who are not progressing in literacy learning. Sometimes just helping children connect with purposeful activity related to literacy will get them moving.

Setting up play situations and observing how children use the materials can provide strong evidence of knowledge. This kind of assessment takes practice. A teacher could begin by jotting down little stories of how students interact with print—perhaps similar to the Kole or the second-grade stories above. Watch for children adopting a meaning-making stance with text—telling stories from text that relate to pictures, carefully writing, even scribbles—and explaining the meaning and use of their text, passing notes to each other, making lists, looking up information in books.

In a classroom, it may be difficult to spend time with every child or to notice little episodes for every child. A more formal way to assess knowledge of purpose of written-language knowledge is to use a simple protocol such as the one in this chapter's appendix A. Meet individually with children and ask the questions on the protocol. Look for evidence that the child has or does not have an understanding of the purposes of written language.

Because children are different, it may be necessary to rework the questions on the interview protocol to meet particular needs.

Summary of Purpose Knowledge and Teaching Strategies

- Children need many experiences with written language, experiences in which print is used for real-life purposes, in contexts that mirror the ways adults use written language.

- Teachers need to call attention to these purposes and show children directly how print is helpful. Understanding the purpose of text provides a foundation and often a motivation for learning to decode.
- In addition, focusing on the meaning of the task helps children develop a *meaning-making stance*. A child who knows that the text is supposed to be meaningful will focus on comprehension from the beginning. It will not be necessary to teach children to "comprehend" later in their school years.

NATURE OF WRITTEN LANGUAGE

The second knowledge component is understanding the nature of written language. Knowing the purpose of written language is necessary but not sufficient for developing literacy skills. Children must also come to understand how our English writing system works. What are the relevant features?

Written language is a system of symbols that represents aspects of oral language. In English, letters represent sounds that combine (sometimes in a regular fashion, often not regularly) to form words. Words are represented by groups of letters separated from each other on the page by spaces. Groups of words form sentences marked by capital letters and periods.

There is nothing intuitive about this system. It is arbitrary, developed over time by consensus of groups of people. Children must learn (reinvent, in Vygotsky's terms) the conventions of this system. Here are several of the conventions that need to be learned early in the development process:

1. *Written language in books often has a distinctive sound, different phrasing, sentence structures, and grammar from oral language.* A greater variety of words is used in written language than in most oral language. For example, "Once upon a time" is not often heard in verbal conversation.

All children speak some type of dialect in their homes. These dialects often do not match the more formal grammar and vocabulary of written text. Children who have not heard much written language may have difficulty predicting words in print when they try to read. Children who say and hear others say, "I seen my friend at the park," may not recognize the word "saw," which would be more likely in a print version of that sentence.

2. *Books follow certain conventions.* They have a front cover and a back cover. Reading begins at the front cover and progresses page by page through the book. The book needs to be right-side up, usually first recognized because of pictures in books. Children who understand how books work in this way are sometimes considered to be "book aware."

Noah is Susan's three-year-old brother. Noah has watched as Susan interacts with books. He will then pick up books, turn to the front cover, and turn the pages one by one. Sometimes he labels pictures; sometimes he just sort of "mumbles" something for each page. He is book aware.

3. *Pictures in books are related to the meaning of the text, but "words" carry the meaning.* Children who recognize the difference between pictures and printed symbols are said to be "print aware." It sometimes takes a while for young children to realize that the squiggly lines on the page actually tell the story.

Kole will point to and name pictures of his beloved cars, trucks, trains, and planes in one of his books. The pictures are all labeled. When asked to point to the "words" in the text, he chooses the printed words. When asked, "What does this word say?" he will name the appropriate vehicle.

So, he seems to know that words are special symbols—separate from pictures, at least—and that the words in this type of book are connected directly to the pictures. Is he actually reading the words? Not in the sense adults mean because there are other concepts to be learned. But he is progressing in his knowledge of the nature of written language. Earlier in the year, he had named pictures but did not know about words.

4. *"First" has particular meanings in written language.* The first letter of a word is the letter on the left. The first word in a sentence is the one with a capital letter. The first paragraph is the one on top. Knowing about left to right and top to bottom is called "directionality."

The left-hand page is read first, then the right. Reading begins at the topmost line of print and progresses to the bottom and then on to the next page. We read from left to right on each line, doing a "return sweep" at the end of each line.

It is not uncommon for children who have learned to write the letters in their names to sometimes write them from right to left or to reverse the letters. This is a normal part of directionality learning for kindergarteners and some first graders.

Directionality is a concept that is so obvious to accomplished readers that adults may forget that children have to "notice" this relevant feature. Unless someone explicitly shows children the importance of direction, they may not notice on their own. Imagine how confusing instruction would be for a child who does not have knowledge of directionality.

5. *Letters are consistent in shape and direction.* Capital and lowercase letters might look exactly alike or completely different. Orientation on the page is important, a relevant feature for identifying letters, especially for specific letters that differ only in orientation. The letters "b," "p," "d," and "q" are all made with the same pen strokes. The orientation determines which letter is which.

It is important to note that before interacting with printed symbols, a child's world is full of three-dimensional objects. It does not matter which way we hold a fork, it is still a fork. When it is turned sideways, it does not become a "plate"; it is not a "cup" if held upside down. With three-dimensional objects, orientation is not important to identification.

However, orientation is very important with two-dimensional written symbols. Some children miss this relevant feature and need some explicit instruction. Children who confuse "b" and "d" are not dealing with a brain deficiency. They simply need some instruction on directionality.

There are limited ways to make the letters and there are only twenty-six letters, so learning the letters is not a tremendously difficult task. But it is very important that adults understand what features are relevant in written symbols and point them out to children.

Someone has shown Kole how to write his name, and he can recognize the letters from his name in other print environments. He does not name all the letters yet, but he knows that the letters have specific forms. He will say, "That's my name," when he sees the letter "k" in another word. He is just beginning to know how to look at letters and to know what lines are important—a relevant feature—for identifying letters. He recognizes the "o" and calls it an "o," but he calls the "l" a "straight up." Little by little he is working out the features of print in his four-year-old way of thinking.

6. *Words that have the same letters—in the same order—are the same words*. Many teachers have noticed that some children will read a word correctly on one page and then misread or be stymied by the same word on the next page. The problem often is lack of understanding that one relevant feature for a word is the order of the letters.

Michelle, a first-grade student in tutoring, did not have this understanding. It was common for her to read a word on one page and then not recognize it on the next page. By showing her the same word in different situations, and guiding "discovery" that the words were the same (comparing the words letter by letter or building them with magnetic letters), the teacher was able to facilitate the learning of other "sight" words.

Until she knew what "same word" meant, Michelle was very inconsistent in learning her list of "sight words." One has to wonder what she was focusing on as she tried to memorize those words—first letter, length of word, shape of word?

A little focused instruction was enough to help Michelle move forward. If the teacher had not noticed this lack of understanding, Michelle might still have figured it out eventually, but she will progress much more smoothly because the teacher noticed and took time to help her understand the concept. (Also see the story of Jimmy in appendix C.)

Another "word" issue for some children is confusion between the terms "word" and "letter." Imagine how confused a child would be if the teacher said, "What is the first word?" and the child was actually looking at the first "letter."

7. *Spoken language is made up of units called "words."* These are not always clearly differentiated in speech. We say, "Gonnagitcha," in one blended utterance, even though the actual sentence contains four words, "Going to get you."

If a child can break individual words from oral text, we say the child can do *auditory segmentation of words.* ***This one concept is probably most responsible for delaying young children as they learn to read.*** Early readers should be helped to aurally break sentences into words—probably without written forms in the beginning.

Imagine what would happen in a typical classroom situation. Children are "reading" together out loud. If a particular child does not understand how to separate spoken words from speech, how will he accomplish matching the spoken word to written word, which is needed to participate meaningfully in the activity?

This concept is about having a conceptual knowledge of what "word" means. The visual part—symbol separated by spaces—is relatively easy to learn. Separating individual spoken words requires children to think about "words" as something apart from their meaning. "The dog" is one idea to children, and in fact, "the" is often not verbalized distinctly but is blended with the noun to follow. The fact that it is two words will need to be learned by some children.

Once simple books are presented, children should point to words in the text and aurally segment the words to match the symbols. Without the understanding of auditory segmentation of words, children will be confused by the matching process, matching spoken words to written words in text.

8. *Individual words are made up of a series of sounds* that again are not generally differentiated in speech. This is a very abstract concept. In fact, many words cannot really be segmented. If you try to say the individual sounds of the word "cat," /kuh/a/tuh/, and then blend them together—if you are faithful to the sounds—you will not get the word "cat." The /kuh/a/tuh/ will never come together as "cat" until alterations are made in the sounds to blend them. The extra /uh/ that we need to pronounce individual sounds is not present in the spoken word.

If a child understands that spoken words are subdivided into sounds, we say that child is "phonemically aware." This is an important concept in early literacy, but not as important as auditory segmentation of words from the speech stream. Children with some level of phonemic awareness will find it easier to match sounds and letters.

Some children develop this concept *before* they learn to read; some become phonemically aware *as* they learn to read; and some only understand the concept *after* they have become fluent readers. (About 30 percent of my college students each semester cannot pass a test of phonemic awareness without instruction.)

Activities for Developing Concepts of the Nature of Written Language

- Do shared reading of big books or charts pointing to words and reading word by word. Encourage students to take turns reading and pointing to the words. After you read, point out the features of words, "This word starts like David's name," "This word has three letters," or "Look how long this word is." Use the terms "word" and "letter" and make sure children understand the terms. Note: In all these activities remember to maintain the meaning-making stance.
- Use a mask (a sticky tab the right size to cover an individual word in your text) to cover selected words in familiar shared readings. Ask the children to predict what word has been covered.
- Give children a frame (a piece of cardboard with a cut-out the size of a word in your text; a handle makes it easier to hold) and ask them to find particular words in familiar shared readings and frame them. As a variation, ask them to find two words that are the same, or two words that start the same, or two words with six letters, and so on. If the targeted words are not sight words, children should be taught to reread the page to find out what the word says. In this way, they will learn to use their knowledge of the text to decode a word. Note: The frame helps to focus attention and allows the teacher to understand what the child is thinking.
- Make sentence strips for shared readings. At first make the print on the strips exactly match the book or chart print. Ask children to match the strips to the original print and then reread the page to tell what the strip says. They can also use the strips in a pocket chart to rebuild the story. This encourages them to discover that words with the same letters in the same order are the same word.
- Make a second set of sentence strips and cut them into word cards. Have children match these words to the strips or to the original story, and then read the words. Have them rebuild sentences or the whole story with the cards. At this stage, children should have the whole text available for reference.
- Do shared writing in which children dictate sentences for the teacher to write. Encourage them to dictate the sentences word by word. Pause after writing a word and wait for *one* more word. You will be encouraging children to break their sentences into individual words. It may help to first

draw a line for each word the children suggest. (Children who do not repeat the same sentence, but go on with the story, will need lots of practice dictating. Those are children who do not know what words are auditorily.)

- Make name and concept books and encourage children to practice reading them. A name book is a little eight-page homemade book with the child's name written on each page. On some pages, it is written once, on other pages it is written twice, three, or four times. It allows the child to read a word he/she knows and practice one-to-one. As children learn each other's names, they can then practice reading each other's books. A concept book is in the same format but uses words that mean something to the child; for example, one child had a "Barbie" book because of her interest in Barbie dolls. Children can make these books for each other.

- Work with the leveled pattern books in a Marie Clay–type guided reading. Be sure to give strong introductions and scaffold the use of one-to-one correspondence. Have children point to words as they read. Until one-to-one is consistent, children may only memorize the books and develop inappropriate ideas of the reading process, so it may be more appropriate to use other reading as noted above, especially if your supply of leveled books is limited.

One conclusion that researchers frequently draw from studies of the efficacy of various literacy teaching methods is that the most important variable for children learning to read is the insightfulness of the teacher. Some have concluded that it is the only variable that is consistent through different studies (Pressley, Allington, Wharton-McDonald, Collins-Block, and Morrow 2001).

As you use these activities with young children, remember that it is very important to observe children and continually assess their understanding of "nature of written language" concepts. Matching the right activity with the child(ren) who needs it is critical.

Vygotsky (1962) suggests that learning happens in the Zone of Proximal Development (see theory box). The teacher as the More Knowledgeable Other is responsible for determining what individual children understand at a particular time and providing appropriate activities, explanations, and modeling that will help the child move forward. This is particularly important for the 20 percent because they have not benefited from whatever has happened in classrooms thus far.

Read the story of Jimmy and the story of Nathan (appendixes C and D) to see examples of how the teacher was able to provide what was needed at the right moment to help the child progress.

THEORY BOX: VYGOTSKY

Vygotsky (1962) used the term "Zone of Proximal Development" to explain how adults and children interact in a teaching situation.

The *bottom* of the "Zone" is what children know or can do on their own. The *top* of the "Zone" is what children can do with the support of a more knowledgeable other—a teacher, a parent, a peer with more understanding.

The job of the MKO (more knowledgeable other) is to provide tasks that allow the learner to use what the learner already knows, but also allows for some new learning. Finding the right challenge—staying in the zone—is the first job of the MKO.

Another important job is to point out critical features that the learner may be overlooking.

Assessing Children's Knowledge of the Nature of Written Language

As in assessment for "purpose of written language" concepts, one of the best assessments is observation and careful note-taking. Keep individual notebooks or a card system for each child who seems to lack understanding of some aspect of the nature of print. Date the cards and review them regularly. When you share one of the activities listed above with groups of children, watch your targeted student for evidence of understanding or lack of understanding.

In appendix B is a Concepts of Print inventory that could be used to evaluate these concepts periodically. The inventory requires a student to interact with a simple text. Using this inventory may help a teacher build an understanding of these concepts.

WHAT HAPPENS NEXT?

The concepts of the purpose and nature of written language as described above are critical to early literacy development in young children and can create roadblocks for children when they are not understood. Confusion caused by misinterpretation of purpose and nature can persist for quite a while if it is not caught and corrected.

The two stories in the appendixes are true stories that show how such problems were recognized and addressed. In one story the intervention was successful because it happened in a summer session. There was no competition between approaches. In Jimmy's story, the intervention showed progress but was short-circuited by choices made by instructors not knowledgeable about the importance of purpose and nature concepts.

The prevailing approach to teaching decoding and encoding follows a behaviorist, task-analysis approach. That means that children are taught letter/sound correspondences often out of context of real reading. Some methods actually try to teach complicated sets of phonics rules and all their exceptions to five- and six-year-olds. More common are workbook pages of drill and practice on consonants, blends, digraphs, short vowels, long vowels, and so on.

It is not uncommon to find kindergarteners who can tell you sounds for particular letters but do not use that knowledge to help them read. Why does that happen?

Of course, many children make this connection. Who are the children who understand? They are children who understand the purpose and nature of written language and who have a *meaning-making stance*. They have learned to see reading and writing as problem-solving activities with the goal to obtain or create a meaning. These children can deal with the irregularities of the written language system because they see the bigger picture. That is, they know personally relevant purposes for written language and understand basic features of the print system.

The 20 percent are not so fortunate. Without an understanding of why and how the system works, these children struggle with nonsensical tasks (out-of-context phonics drills, decodable texts with little meaning) that do not bring them closer to the goal of being fluent readers with a meaning-making stance. Literacy is not seen as a tool for learning by these children, but as an end in itself.

CONCLUSION

When a teacher or a parent says a child is "having difficulty" or "having problems" learning to read, the teacher has not told us how to help the child.

If the problem is a slow start, the teacher will provide meaningful print activities and allow more time for development. If the child has had no exposure to print, the teacher will read to that child and engage the child in lots of meaningful print activities. If the child sees no reason to learn to read, the teacher will help the child find personally relevant reasons. If the child has specific confusions about the nature of print, the teacher will provide in-context, explicit instruction on the concepts needed. Approaching every child with the same remedies would be inappropriate and a waste of time. A teacher must begin by identifying issues that are unique to the child.

All children need a knowledgeable, skillful teacher who understands the literacy process and how to provide support to children using multiple techniques and methods designed for each child's understanding of the literacy process at any given time. (That understanding can change moment to moment.)

The Early Literacy Framework is an attempt to empower teachers of young children with knowledge of the importance and complexity of early literacy learning. The concepts, assessments, and activities described can be used by teachers:

- To support all children's learning in the classroom. Learning related to purpose of print and developing a "meaning-making stance" is beneficial to all children regardless of literacy knowledge and skills.
- To prevent complications that can arise from children's confusions and reduce the 20 percent.
- To identify children who have specific areas of need. Addressing these confusions in the context of meaningful literacy experiences will allow children to *own* the meaning-making process and make use of regular classroom instruction (see Nathan's story in appendix D).

The "light bulb" will eventually come on for almost all children at some point, with or without appropriate instruction. What has been done with that child before the defining "aha" experiences will determine the eventual outcome for that child. Nathan (appendix D) received appropriate interventions at the right time and was able to progress more or less normally. Jimmy (appendix C), on the other hand, could be on a path to a disability label. He has already *labeled himself* as "not a reader." What happens in the future will depend on the insightfulness of subsequent teachers.

For all children, but especially for the 20 percent, the quick-fix, one-method-fits-all, assembly-line approach to literacy instruction has never been successful and never will be because children are not automobiles to be built all the same on an assembly line. They are more like finely crafted, hand-made pottery, each one similar but unique. "The 20 Percent Solution" is a master-teacher's hand.

APPENDIX A: PURPOSE OF WRITTEN LANGUAGE INTERVIEW

Student's Name: Date: Interviewer:

1. Who do you know who can read?
2. What are some things that person reads?
3. Why do people read?

  Use follow-up questions to get as many answers as possible. If the student just lists things for question #2, ask specifically about that reading. (For example, if the student says her mother reads the mail, ask why.)

  If "why" questions get no response, try asking "when." When does your mother read the mail?

4. Who do you know who writes? What are some things that person writes?
5. Why do people write? Again, "when" questions may work better.
6. If responses are not forthcoming, try describing a scenario and ask what might be read or written. Choose a place that would be familiar to the child.

  For example:
  Do you go to the grocery store?
  What do people read at the grocery store?

Which statement describes the child's recognition of reading/writing behaviors in this interview?

  3—Child recognizes and can describe reading behaviors in multiple contexts
  2—Child recognizes reading/writing behaviors in limited contexts
  1—Child cannot name or describe any reading behaviors

Which statement describes the child's understanding of purposes of print during this interview?

3—Child identifies multiple purposes for reading and writing, giving many examples

2—Child identifies some purposes with a few examples

1—Child does not identify any purposes for reading /writing behavior

Additional information: Watch as the student interacts with books. Write a quick note when you see signs of understanding purpose of print. Be sure to date it.

APPENDIX B: CONCEPTS OF PRINT CHECKLIST (SIMILAR TO CLAY)

Child's name: Date: Examiner:

For this assessment, you will read a short book to the child, asking him or her the questions as listed. Choose a book with one or two sentences on a page.

Make a checkmark if the child gives an appropriate answer. Write notes as well, particularly if the child responds in an unexpected way.

1. Before reading, hand the book to the child upside down and backward. See if the child turns it to the correct position for reading.
2. Say, "Show me the front of the book."
3. Say, "Show me the back of the book."
4. Say, "Point to the title."
5. Say, "Which page do we read first?"
6. Say, "Which part tells the story? Which part do people read?" (Look for the child to choose the print, not the pictures.)Read the story to the child. Enjoy the reading. Talk about the meaning. Take notes on the child's response to the book.
7. Go back and read the first page and point to the words as you read. Ask the child to read what you just read and point to the words. Note whether the child points to each word and matches voice to print.
8. Find a page that has more than one line of print. Again, read and point to the words, and ask the child to do the same. Does the child move left to right and include a return sweep?
9. Find a page with several words on it. Ask the child to draw a circle with her finger around a "word." Find an appropriate page and give the following directions:
10. "Find two words that are the same."
11. "Find the first word on this page."
12. "Find the last word on this page."

13. "Put two fingers around a letter." Then, "Put two fingers around a word." Go back and forth between "word" and "letter" a few times.
14. Point to five different letters and ask the child to name them. Choose "b/d, n/u, m/w" where orientation is important.
15. "Show me a capital letter."
16. "Show me a lowercase letter."
17. "Show me a period." Tell the student, "I'm going to say a word and I want you to break the word apart." Do the following as a practice item, "mom" /m/o/m/.
18. she (2)
19. red (3)
20. sat (3)

Total (20)

APPENDIX C: THE CASE OF JIMMY

Jimmy was a six-year-old who had just finished kindergarten and was referred to a reading clinic by his parents. They were concerned that he was not learning to read. The kindergarten teacher stated that Jimmy had not learned all his letter names, refused to write, and did not know his list of sight words.

In an initial interview at the reading clinic, Jimmy knew many letter names and a few sight words and could handle a book correctly—starting at the beginning and turning page by page. He also knew where the "words" were on the page, as opposed to pictures and page numbers.

WHERE DO BUGS LIVE?

Bugs live in trees.
Bugs live in water.
Bugs live in dirt.
Bugs live in grass.
Bugs have many habitats.

Jimmy was given a predictable pattern story called "Where Do Bugs Live?" Mrs. Jones read the title and talked through the book with him, saying the words on each page and calling attention to the picture clues to the whereabouts of the bugs.

Jimmy was interested in the text and added comments throughout. Then she read the first page and had Jimmy read it after her. He was able to repeat while pointing to the words, showing auditory segmentation of words at some level. Then he was asked to read the next page using the pattern and the picture clues. He began spelling the words—"B, n, g, s."

Mrs. Jones asked him to read the first page again. He read "Bugs live in trees" without difficulty but proceeded to misspell the word "bugs" on the next page. Mrs. Jones made a hypothesis that Jimmy did not understand that the same letters in the same order are the same word. On that basis, she asked him to look at the two words letter by letter. He checked the words for the same letters, still calling the "u" an "n." Finally, he said, "These are the same."

Mrs. Jones said, "If this word on the first page is 'bugs,' what is this word on the second page?" Jimmy thought for a moment and then said, "Bugs," very triumphantly. Apparently, this concept was new to him. On each page after that, he checked the word "bugs" with the "bugs" on the first page, and the lesson was learned.

Jimmy checked the word "live" on his own and read it correctly on each page. The last word on each page was read using the picture for a clue. Mrs. Jones had to help with some of these words since Jimmy did not know enough letter/sound correspondences to work them out by himself if the pictures were not explicit enough.

The fact that Jimmy called the "u" an "n" was noted but not dealt with at the time. Mrs. Jones felt that interrupting the flow of the story to correct a letter name would not be useful. Jimmy is already heavily focused on bits of knowledge.

Following the initial session, Mrs. Jones continued to work with Jimmy two or three days a week for about six weeks. They followed Marie Clay's Reading Recovery format (Clay, 1993), rereading familiar books, taking running records, introducing new books, and writing a sentence.

In a lesson a few weeks into instruction, as Jimmy learned more letter/ sound correspondences from the context and from writing, he was able to self-correct in the "Bugs" book. (It remained a favorite book. He said it was the first book he ever read, and he wanted to read it every session.) He read "Bugs live in hills" when the sentence read "Bugs live in dirt." The teacher waited, and Jimmy tracked the word "dirt" (ran his finger under the word) and read the sentence again correctly. He said, "It can't be 'hills' because it starts like my last name, Dawson."

A month later, Jimmy was reading one of his books as usual when he stopped and wrote the word "good" on a piece of paper. (Apparently Jimmy's teacher had written that word on his paper. The fact that he was interested in this was pretty exciting.)

"I thought you said 'oo' says /oo/ (as in 'too')," he said to Mrs. Jones rather indignantly. The teacher said, "Yes, that is one of the sounds of 'oo.'" Jimmy showed her "good" and read the word. Mrs. Jones asked what the sound of "oo" was in that word, and Jimmy replied correctly.

Mrs. Jones said, "That's the other sound for 'oo.' There are two of them." Jimmy looked a little incredulous. They were sitting in the hallway of the school and there were several notices hanging on the wall. One was about the need for "classroom" parents to make "cookies" for the upcoming "school" picnic. There was another notice about the "book" fair that was coming up.

Mrs. Jones showed each word to Jimmy and had him try to say each word with first one sound for "oo" and then the other. He said each word with both sounds and was quickly able to choose the correct word. Jimmy had begun to notice the patterns in sound/symbol correspondences and also learned a strategy for using his knowledge—try different sounds until you get a meaningful word.

Jimmy was also learning sight words—some of his favorites were "special" and "habitat." He remembered the longer, more meaningful words easily, recognizing them in different contexts. Some more common words took longer to recognize consistently.

As he read, Jimmy often would stop and talk about the text he was reading. He had a great deal of knowledge and loved explaining something from the text or perhaps arguing with the text. In other words, Jimmy had a "meaning-making stance" from the beginning.

Unfortunately, the association with the reading clinic came to an end. It was decided in the school that Jimmy should be referred to the reading specialist, who began a rule-based phonics-first reading program with him. When Mrs. Jones visited him later in the year, he was busily trying to sound out words and spouting rules about "guardian consonants." He was no longer using his knowledge of the world and multiple strategies to decode text.

Perhaps even more unfortunate is that Jimmy no longer felt successful. Reading was not an interesting task that opened up new ideas. He told Mrs. Jones that he was sure he would never learn to read.

APPENDIX D: THE STORY OF NATHAN

Nathan was a seven-year-old who had just finished first grade. His mother was concerned that he was not reading and brought him to a reading clinic. The mother explained that he had attended kindergarten and had learned phonics but could not read.

Nathan was asked by the clinician to read a short text. Nathan began, "/t/ / h/ /e/ /b/ /o/ /y/ /i/ /s/," producing sounds, one by one. Mr. Barnett stopped Nathan and asked, "What are you doing?" Nathan responded, "Reading."

Mr. Barnett decided to try a different tactic. He asked Nathan to tell him something he had done that day. Nathan responded, "I played basketball."

"That's great," said Mr. Barnett. "I'm going to write that down." He wrote the word "I," stopped, and looked at Nathan. Nathan was confused, but responded, "I played basketball."

Mr. Barnett said, "I," pointing to the word, and then wrote "played" and paused again for Nathan to complete the sentence. Once again, Nathan repeated the whole sentence.

Mr. Barnett finished the sentence and then read it back, pointing to each word and pausing between words. When Nathan was asked to read the sentence, he quickly repeated his sentence again. When asked to point to the words as he read, Nathan disgustedly ran his finger across the whole sentence with no one-to-one correspondence between spoken and written words.

Mr. Barnett hypothesized that Nathan did not understand that sentences we speak can be broken into individual words. He also suggested that Nathan did not know any other strategies but sounding out, and that he did not have a meaning-making stance related to text.

Over the course of the next few weeks of lessons, Mr. Barnett read aloud to Nathan from books that Nathan selected. The two of them discussed Nathan's interests—mostly sports in the beginning. It was clear that Nathan was very knowledgeable and had good language skills. Mr. Barnett discovered that Nathan was used to being read to; his mother read him his favorite books regularly.

Each day that they met, Mr. Barnett had Nathan dictate a sentence, helping him learn to segment the oral sentence and match to the written words. Finally, one day, after about three weeks, Nathan read the sentence back, pointing to the words one at a time, looked incredulously at Mr. Barnett, and said, "Hey, that's what I said." (The "aha" moment.)

Nathan had learned important concepts about the purpose and nature of written language. From then on, he progressed quickly. All his previously learned phonics knowledge was now useful when applied as one of several strategies to make meaning from text.

Nathan left the summer tutoring program reading at a second-grade level on Informal Reading Inventories, and started the next year in second grade.

After about the first month of second grade, Nathan's mother called Mr. Barnett. "Nathan is in trouble again." Mr. Barnett asked what the problem was, and his mother said that he was not getting his work done. The teacher thought he might have a learning disability.

Mr. Barnett arranged to visit the classroom. The desks were set in a "U" shape, with a reading circle at the open end of the "U." While Mr. Barnett was observing, the teacher was working with a reading group and reading an interesting story. Nathan was at the end of one of the arms of the "U" and could hear the story. He really enjoyed being read to, so he was listening to the story instead of working.

Mr. Barnett asked Nathan what he was supposed to be doing. Nathan looked around at his classmates and said, "I don't know." Mr. Barnett took Nathan to the whiteboard. In the corner was written an assignment. After the text was pointed out, and its purpose explained, Nathan read the assignment easily. "Oh," he said, "I didn't know about that."

Nathan and Mr. Barnett went back to his seat. Nathan looked at the board, got out the appropriate workbook, and turned to the correct page. There he looked perplexed. Mr. Barnett asked him how he could solve his problem. Nathan could not suggest any solutions. Mr. Barnett showed him the red print on the top of the page. Nathan said, "Oh, I never read that red stuff." "Well, read it now," said Mr. Barnett.

Nathan read the directions and was amazed. He immediately got to work and finished quickly.

Figuring out relevant features was not always one of Nathan's strengths. He needed support learning what was important in new situations. Now that the teacher and his mother knew what to look for, Nathan did well.

When Nathan was in sixth grade, his mother wrote Mr. Barnett a letter. She wanted him to know that Nathan was still doing well with reading and other assignments.

REFERENCES

Clay, M. M. (1993). *Reading recovery: A guidebook for teachers in training.* Portsmouth, NH: Heinemann.

Downing, J. (1970). Children's concepts of language in learning to read. *Education Research, 12*, 106–12.

Meltzer, N. S., & Herse, R. (1969). The boundaries of written words as seen by first graders. *Journal of Reading Behavior, 1*, 3–14.

Piaget, J. (1995). *The essential Piaget.* Northvale, NJ: Jason Aronson Inc.

Pressley, M., Allington, R. L., Wharton-McDonald, R., Collins-Block, C., & Morrow, L. (2001). *Learning to read: Lessons from exemplary first-grade classrooms.* New York: Guilford.

Reid, J. F. (1966). Learning to think about reading. *Educational Research, 9,* 56–62.

Sawyer, D. J. (1992). *Test of awareness of language segments (TALS).* Austin, TX: PRO-ED.

Sulzby, E. (1985). Children's emergent reading of favorite storybooks: A developmental study. *Reading Research Quarterly, 20,* 458–81.

Vygotsky, L. S. (1962). *Thought and language.* Cambridge, MA: MIT Press.

Teaching Memoir: Kangaroos

Arielle Suggs

Growing up, I liked to believe that my teachers had computers for brains. Teachers knew everything, or so it appeared. One of the things that I always admired about my teachers was the way they delivered information in such a confident and intelligent manner. Students dared not challenge anything they said, thus giving the *illusion* that they knew everything. I never actually heard a teacher say, "I don't know," or leave a student's question unanswered.

As a teacher candidate with this perception of teachers in mind, I was always hard on myself when it came to perfecting content knowledge. Sure, teachers have to be knowledgeable, but I would pressure myself until I reached what I thought was perfection. After all, I wanted to be a good teacher.

It was not until the fall of my sophomore year in college that I was able to release the pressure to be perfect, and it all started with a class of bright first-grade students. On Wednesdays, as a part of a field experience requirement for an education class, I read aloud picture books I thought the students would enjoy.

This particular Wednesday, I was extremely excited because I was reading one of my favorite children's books, *Is Your Mama a Llama?* by Deborah Guarino. I appreciated the rhythm and humor of the story and I was confident that the first graders, whom I had come to know very well during previous weeks, would love this story as much as I did. I was correct. They asked me to read it again, and I did.

After I read the story, the students and I had a brief discussion and then I opened the floor to questions. The first little boy I called on had a question about the kangaroo at the end of the book. "How many baby kangaroos can the mommy carry in her pouch?" he asked. I had no idea.

His question then provoked a series of kangaroo questions from the other students. Not only did I not know the answer to his question, but I was honestly unable to answer any of the other questions that the students had about kangaroos. I was worried that I would lose their respect and trust because I did not know the answers. My mind began shuffling for any information on kangaroos, or at least a smooth and sophisticated way to say, "I don't know."

Finally, I said, "Hmm, that's a great question. We should research it!"

The classroom teacher turned around from her desk to say, "That's a good idea, we'll go to the computer lab after lunch."

The kids became excited and suddenly I was not so embarrassed. While the students were at lunch, I talked with the teacher about how frantic I had become when the students began to ask questions about kangaroos. I told her that if only I had known that they were going to ask these questions, I would have done research on kangaroos before I came to class.

"How were you to know?" she said, "I didn't even know." She further explained to me that in the classroom things do not always go the way they are planned and sometimes the best lesson is one that takes advantage of students' interests. "You have a chance here to build on what the first graders already know about kangaroos, and teach them something new."

After speaking with her I realized that I'm only human. Teachers are also students and should continue to learn throughout their lives. Teachers do not have computers for brains.

Now, I'm not so hard on myself. If there is something I do not know, there is no need to panic. I can always learn it alongside my students.

Chapter Three

Students Won't Read Textbooks? Try Three-Point Book Club

Jamie Whitman-Smithe

Teachers—of elementary, middle, secondary, postsecondary, and also adult basic education—do not despair! After reading this chapter you will realize how easy it will be to adapt Three-Point Book Club to any grade level, and moreover, after implementing this technique, you will find that your students can and will read the assigned texts that you require in your class.

The only prerequisites are, first, there must be assigned readings in your class, and second, there must be students who may not want to read the assigned texts! The Three-Point Book Club has been used successfully by the author and will provide you with a teaching technique that has been tested repeatedly in various classrooms.

Practicing constructivist teachers believe that in order for learning to take place, teachers must provide environments that afford students multiple opportunities to take in and organize new information. They also believe that students experiencing these environments will execute tasks, projects, and performances—thus providing evidence of being able to internalize and retrieve information that will be used to solve problems in varying formats. Three-Point Book Club is a teaching technique that illustrates how teachers who espouse the constructivist philosophy of teaching develop knowledge-construction experiences for students.

This chapter chronicles the process of developing teaching techniques that one constructivist teacher has used (and presently uses) to support the constructivist philosophy in classrooms.

FIRST TECHNIQUE

Historical Backdrop

Years ago a professor (chair of the pharmacology department at a major university) realized that due to the nature of his discipline, textbooks were not a reliable source for updating his graduate and postdoctoral students on the latest research. To remedy the situation the professor created *Journal Club*. Journal Club met fifty-two weeks of the year (including summer and Christmas vacations) unless the professor was out of town.

Each week the professor provided his students with three current journal articles to prepare for discussion; the graduate and postgraduate students took turns presenting these articles to the group. After the presentation of each article, a lively discussion would ensue.

The personal discipline required by each student to read and prepare the journal articles weekly, in addition to the social aspect of the professor's Journal Club, impressed a graduate student in education. Thus, a mental note was made by the graduate student in education to someday create a similar Journal Club exercise and introduce it into the classroom environment to promote knowledge construction.

Years later, this graduate-student-turned-teacher-educator implemented a unique version of the Journal Club. The assignments were less difficult: undergraduate education students were required to read and answer specific questions about four assigned journal articles during the semester.

Even though the students enjoyed Journal Club, eventually the exercise was discontinued because it became clear that this assignment was too easy. Reflecting on the assignment, the teacher realized that while asking students to read journal articles and answer a specific set of questions would fit comfortably into a traditional classroom setting, it did not adhere to constructivist practices.

SECOND TECHNIQUE

Shortly after the Journal Club came to an end, the idea for another type of gathering emerged; the new club would be more beneficial to students and would help teachers ensure that assigned readings would actually be read.

The requirements for the Three-Point Book Club are as follows:

1. Students are to read the chapters assigned for the week and *choose* one of the chapters to write about for class.

2. Next, students reread the *chosen* chapter and decide what they believe to be the three Most Important Points (MIPs) in the chapter (marginalia is encouraged).
3. Students analyze each point and explain *why they believe* each point is important.
4. Of these three points, students *choose* one point that they believe to be the MIP and mark the point with an asterisk.
5. Students then answer two questions:

   a. "Why is this point important for us to know at this time in our lives?"
   b. "How can we begin to integrate this point into our lives?"

6. Within groups, students discuss why this point is the MIP. (Students are assured that there is not an answer key that lists the correct important points for each chapter. Eventually students realize that this exercise provides them with an opportunity to express their opinions in a nonjudgmental setting.)

GROUP WORK

The next part of the Three-Point Book Club involves group work. On the day the reading assignments are due, students are instructed to retain their papers and to sit in groups (sometimes preassigned and sometimes not). Each group chooses a leader. Group members are instructed to read their Three-Point-Book Club assignments to their fellow group members, and with group consensus, they choose an MIP from all of the MIPs that have been read.

Finally, the group discusses the current MIP and includes as justification why the group believes the MIP is important for students at this moment in their lives. During group work students begin to realize the answers they have generated prior to class differ from the answers they have generated within their groups because of the varying viewpoints of group members. Furthermore, in order for group members to come to a consensus, they must develop a system for collaboration, such as listening to group members' differing views in a respectful manner or summarizing group comments.

After each group has shared its views with the class, the teacher asks the class to look up at the board (where all MIPs have been written) and decide if one MIP seems more important than all of the other MIPs, and if so, why? Sometimes an MIP becomes a *hot* topic. For example, a few years ago, the topic of school uniforms was identified as an important point from an assigned reading. Candidates began a lively discussion: some for uniforms and some against.

After all points have been discussed, one more question is asked that either has been planned ahead of time or has come to the teacher's mind during class. The question is introduced with the statement, "Now that our minds are all warmed up, there is one more question." An example of questions (taken from subject matter that pertains to the assigned reading for the day) that have sparked discussion at the end of the class is the following: "Should teenage mothers be allowed to continue their high school education?" The discussion that ensues is often unpredictable!

During the last Three-Point Book Club of the semester, the students are asked to think of a classroom risk they might take and write it at the bottom of their papers. This risk might involve each student participating in some way they had not tried before, such as volunteering to be the leader, expressing an opinion in group, letting other group members do the talking, arguing a point, or writing on the board.

With respect to group work, even though directions are provided, some students still do not understand what is expected of them when they write their responses for Three-Point Book Club. However, during group work not only do students have a chance to read their papers to each other, but they also have a chance to compare their work to their groupmates' work and make changes if necessary. Students have commented that it seems as if they are teaching themselves.

If this same assignment was being incorporated in a traditional classroom, students might be required to study MIPs that the teacher or the textbook previously identified. In this particular context, the students' personal opinions might not be considered important. However, constructivists would recognize the Three-Point Book Club assignment as a knowledge construction exercise because the learning environment is prepared for the students to do the following:

- Choose (given their life and academic experience) what they believe to be the most important point.
- Illustrate their choice with an analytical statement that explains why the point is important.
- Discuss with their group all the points chosen by members and from these choose the most MIP and again develop an analytical statement to explain why the point is important.
- Discuss choices in class in a small group and then with the entire class.

SCORING SHEETS

The Three-Point Book Club has been used in three different classroom formats: (1) a class where assigned readings are in four trade books; (2) a class in which assigned readings are in one textbook; and (3) a class where assigned readings are in six trade books. The scoring sheet used with four trade books has been included in appendix A at the end of this chapter.

FINAL STUDENT SELF-ASSESSMENT

For a final exam, students fill out a self-assessment that requires them to reflect on all class assignments. In the Three-Point Book Club section, many students say that they enjoyed the reading assignments because they had the opportunity to share their thoughts and believed they learned new information each time they completed an assignment. Frequently students commented that they had difficulty selecting what they believed to be the three most important points in the readings. Some students note that because of the way the assignment was structured (read, choose three MIPs, choose one MIP, answer questions, be prepared to participate in a group), they believed they could not afford to fall behind in their readings.

Many students surprise themselves by reporting that their curiosity moved them in such a way that they began to enjoy the assigned readings. Others comment that the assignments required a lot of time to read and write. Finally, a few students report surprise when they began to respond creatively when analyzing why a point is important.

The following is an excerpt from the final assessment a student wrote at the end of the first semester that Three-Point Book Club was implemented:

> This particular method of teaching was an excellent idea. Normally[,] if a teacher assigns reading, students do not read unless there is a quiz or a test. This method of teaching [Three-Point Book Club] allows students to read and incorporate their own ideas. [Thus,] they'll be relieved from the normal stress and pressure caused by worry or grades.

After reading this comment the teacher realized that the Three-Point Book Club exercise would become a regular assignment in all courses.

GENERAL OBSERVATIONS

Since students have been challenged with the Three-Point Book Club exercise, the teacher has become aware of the following student behaviors:

- Students will not be successful in group discussions if lessons are inadequately prepared.
- Students desire to impress their group members.
- Students begin to look for unusual MIPs.
- Students freely express opinions, and as a result, group discussions become eloquent.
- Students experience a sense of accomplishment as they demonstrate mastery of reading materials.
- In the beginning of the school year, students submit assignments that are written with misspelled words, incomplete sentences, and incoherent statements. These problems come to light when students read their papers out loud in their groups.
- Students soon begin to experience the responsibility of being required to present their work within a group and begin speaking up and submitting papers that are well written.

CONCLUSION

Each year when Three-Point Book Club is assigned, students' faces communicate, "Are you kidding me?" Students realize that they have to read carefully and diligently if they want to successfully complete the assignment. However, the teacher should remain cognizant of students' abilities and needs. When the assignment was first created, each paper carried a value of ten points and papers were handed in eight times during the semester. During the years changes have been implemented into this assignment. For example, the point value of the papers was raised and the number of papers due each semester was reduced.

It became necessary for the teacher to concentrate on *what a point is* and *what a point is not*. This came about when a colleague began using the club and commented that the students did not know what a point was. This query resulted in the handout entitled *A Point Is* (see appendix B).

Originally, Three-Point Book Club was assigned with the intention of motivating students to complete their required reading assignments. Not only have students completed their assignments, but they have also learned to trust in their choices, explain why they made their choices, participate in peer-editing, learn how to focus when reading, and recognize they are in control of their learning environment. These conclusions can be made because this exercise has been used over the course of a decade.

Teachers who are presently losing sleep because their students do not complete their assigned readings are encouraged to consider using all or parts of the Three-Point Book Club in their elementary, middle, secondary, college, and adult basic-education courses. Teachers who choose to use Three-Point Book Club will enjoy the following results:

- Students who complete all required reading assignments.
- Students who begin to enjoy reading assignments.
- Students who begin to enjoy writing their assignments.
- Teachers who begin to enjoy a good night's sleep!

APPENDIX A

Sample Scoring Sheet for Class with Required Reading from Four Trade Books (50 Points)

> Name (minus 2 pts. if not included)
> Date (minus 2 pts. if not included)
> Name of Book (minus 2 pts. if not included)
> # of Assignment (minus 2 pts. if not included)

Important Point Section Worth a Total of 30 Points

In the first sentence write important point #1. In the next sentence tell the reader why it is one of the most important points (10 pts.).

Write important point #2. In the next sentence tell the reader why it is one of the most important points (10 pts.).

Write important point #3. In the next sentence tell the reader why it is one of the most important points (10 pts.).

{Place asterisk in front of Most Important Point (of the three)—minus 2 pts. if not included.}

Paragraph Section Worth a Total of 20 Points

Begin this paragraph by repeating the most important point (MIP) and describing it (10 pts.). Include in the same paragraph why your MIP is important for us to know at this time in our lives (5 pts.) and how can we begin to integrate this important point into our lives (5 pts.).

APPENDIX B

What Is a Point?

The following includes a definition and an example of a point.

A point is a statement of fact expressed in your own words. For example: Children with disabilities need emotional support.

The following are not points.

- One word. For example: Hobbies.
- A direct quotation. For example: "And so I spent months riding in the rumble seat of my gram's car to and from Westwood and hours sitting in the waiting room, until the day they let us know their findings" (*Al Capone Does My Shirts*, Choldenko, p. 65).
- A definition. For example: Fun is "1. Amusement, esp. lively or playful" (*Oxford Pocket American Dictionary of Current English*, p. 318).
- Summary of the story (from trade books). For example: Temple didn't like the hat she was wearing and caused her mother to get into an automobile accident.

REFERENCES

Choldenko, G. (2004). *Al Capone does my shirts*. New York: G. P. Putnam's Sons.
Oxford Pocket Dictionary of Current English. (2002). New York: Oxford University Press.

Teaching Memoir: The 3 x 4 x 5 Triangle

Thomas B. Cole

My wife and I married later in life. I was about to retire and she was completing her doctorate in education. Much of our conversation focused on her dissertation . . . she used me as a sounding board to think through what she had just written or was about to write. I tried to be patient but had trouble absorbing and understanding her constructivist philosophy of education.

One day after listening to her drone on and on (yes, she was a constructivist zealot), I suddenly smiled and said, "I think that I finally get it! And I have a constructivist story for you." It goes something like this.

Dad wasn't afraid to tackle anything. He grew up on a farm in a time when doing things for yourself was a necessity. But he used resources to plan his work knowledgeably. I remember government pamphlets and reference books around the house on raising chickens, nailing properly, wood-frame construction, fruit-tree spraying, and so forth.

Our family of five lived in three rooms with a path to an outhouse on a couple of acres on the outskirts of town. My parents were just recovering from the Great Depression, but dad was intent on building a new home for us on the property. From sixth grade on I was his apprentice jack-of-all-trades.

We built several structures, including a goat shed and a chicken coop, prior to starting the new house. Each time Dad laid out the footing he would show me how to construct a square corner using a 3 x 4 x 5 triangle.

First, he would establish a front corner of the proposed structure and stretch a string, secured by stakes in the ground, to define the orientation of the front face of the building. Then from the corner he would measure three feet along the string and, using the tape as a protractor, scribe an arc in the dirt underneath the string. Next, he would measure four feet down the side of the proposed structure, at an estimated ninety degrees to the string, and scribe an arc. Then he would measure five feet from just under the string on the three-foot arc and scribe an arc that intersected with the four-foot arc.

Finally, we would stretch a string down the side of the proposed structure so that it was exactly over the intersection of the four-foot and five-foot arcs. For his big finale, Dad would hold his 24" x 16" construction square at the corner of the front and side strings that we had laid out with his 3 x 4 x 5 triangle and prove that our ninety-degree angle was accurate.

Four years later, after I had first learned Dad's practical way to accurately lay out a structure, I started my sophomore year in high school. One of my classes was the dreaded geometry. But as it turned out, I was in heaven! I could mathematically prove Dad's 3 x 4 x 5 triangle, using the Pythagorean theorem. Unlike many of my friends, I thought geometry was the most practical and interesting course I had taken to date.

I went on in math and started my career at a large firm in engineering before computers and calculators were available to do our math for us. Throughout the years, as I calculated fits, distances, and tolerances, I frequently said a silent "thank you" to my father for engaging me in the practicalities of math, as my wife would say, in a very constructivist manner.

Chapter Four

Nature Journaling across the Curriculum

Charmaine M. Herrera

Historians and biographers have long used journals as a tool to gather information about people, places, and key events. For these authors and others, journaling provides a means of reflection. Journaling has been used by cancer patients to reflect upon their experiences, mothers writing in scrapbooks to record family history, travelers to have a record of places visited, and with the extended use of the Internet, "bloggers" can now record their thoughts and reflections on websites that can be accessed by anyone with a computer.

In recent years, educators have "discovered" journaling in many curricular areas such as language arts, science, and math. These journals are used as a way for students to reflect on and explain their thinking and ideas.

NATURE JOURNALS IN THE PAST

Nature journals have been widely used throughout history. Early scientists, artists, and philosophers kept journals that recorded their observations of the natural and cultural world around them. Plato, Copernicus, Michelangelo, Van Gogh, and others used journals as a tool for reflection and description.

In the nineteenth century, the use of nature journals became even more popular with the Naturalist movement that counted in its number Henry David Thoreau, Walt Whitman, and Charles Darwin. Thoreau used his journaling of nature to lead to contemplations of existentialism, government, and other varied topics. Whitman used observations from nature to create poetry that demonstrated his reflections on nature and man. And Darwin collected and described numerous plants and animals during his five-year voyage on the HMS *Beagle* that became the basis of his life's research.

In the present, many hunters, anglers, hikers, and gardeners keep nature journals that allow them to record changes in season, animal populations, stream conditions, and other factors pertinent to their particular interests. Nature journals have a long history of being a tool for reflection, inquiry, and writing.

NATURE JOURNALS IN THE CONSTRUCTIVIST CLASSROOM

Constructivist educators have struggled with which experiences would be most beneficial to students. The goal has always been to teach students how to become critical and creative thinkers that are reflective and inquisitive. Teachers constantly ask themselves if they (the students *and* teachers) are going "deep" enough for real knowledge to be constructed. Science especially provides a challenge.

Inquiry is a hallmark of effective science teaching. However, how to teach the process and practice of inquiry is not always included in traditional educational materials, and with limited time in the day, teachers need to find tools that can integrate all curriculum areas. In this way, students are able to see greater connections throughout the different curriculum areas. Nature journals are one such tool. The steps for using nature journals as a tool for inquiry follow.

In the Classroom

- The first step to using nature journals as an effective tool for curriculum integration is knowledge of curriculum content standards. Core curriculum standards for language arts, math, science, and social studies are being rapidly adopted by many states. Teachers must understand the content that is appropriate for their own classrooms as well as what is required by the school district. Reviewing standards is a way for teachers to identify the content knowledge that their students need to learn and then to think about how nature journaling might incorporate this information.
- After reviewing content and standards, the next step is to choose strategies and skills from various content areas. While at first glance nature journaling seems to fit best in science, essentially that is not true. Nature journaling cuts across the curriculum, easily fitting into art, math, and language arts.

- When teaching in a constructivist manner, it always makes sense to start with what the students already know about the world. With most students in elementary or middle school, the first nature journal entries are drawings, so art integration is a natural point to begin. Shading, depth, lines, texture, and perspective can all be taught as tools to document observations.
- In language arts, teachers can share poetry with the students and discuss how poetry establishes emotions and ideas through words. From there, the teacher can begin to build on the idea of using descriptive language in nature journals. Using class read-alouds to discuss the impact word choice has on writing can help stress the importance of effective communication of ideas through specific and vivid vocabulary. These two key target areas from art and language arts can then be tied together by having the students write poetry in response to nature drawings based on observations.
- Math concepts such as measurement and data analysis are a natural integration point when using nature journals. Students often describe observations through the use of quantitative and qualitative language. For example, they estimate how large or small something is by comparing it to a familiar nonstandard unit such as a thumb or a pencil. This can become the basis of lessons on nonstandard units and their limitations. If trees are a focus of many students' observations in nature journals, the types of measurements (height, circumference) that could be used to give more information about trees become a source of discussion.
- It is important that the inquiry process is overtly taught, which means informing students outright that these concepts will be useful as they document the world around them in their nature journals. Introducing students to the vocabulary associated with inquiry (hypothesis, questioning, observation, data collection, and analysis) helps the students identify themselves as researchers.

Nature journals help students ask questions based on observations that occur naturally through the inquiry process. When questions arise from students' own observations, the questions become relevant and important. The content taught through nature journals becomes understandable to students because the knowledge is based upon the students' own experiences.

In the Field

- The best way to help students begin their nature journals is to get them out in the field. Take a walk around the outside of the school. Venture out into the neighborhood. Visit a nearby pond, field, or nature center, using the resources available in your local area. Equip students with notebooks holding both lined and blank pages, pencils and other drawing utensils, and measurement tools. Then go out and explore!

- Students can draw or describe in words (allow students to begin with the media they feel most comfortable using) anything they see related to nature. This may include plants, animals, insects, or natural resources such as rocks, clouds, water, or soil. Encourage students to get up *close* to observe (observing is more than just looking), and then measure, write, and/or draw what they see.

- Some students may be able to collect items to take back to the classroom, which allows for continued observation. However, for those who draw or describe on the spot, they can later look up their items in a nature guide for further study.

- Back in the classroom, students can get in groups to share their discoveries and ask new questions. The teacher can support them in conversation about the characteristics of their items, the items' roles in nature, and any "preconceived" ideas they may have. Most commonly, students begin to realize they do not have enough data. They need to return to the field and look more closely for details that they didn't see the first time.

- Nature journaling is a process and should be continued in order for students to make comparisons, look for further details, and address those new questions and preconceived notions. For a second nature walk, the teacher can ask students to look for items that they can compare and contrast with the original items in their journals. They may look for more leaves. How do sizes, colors, shapes, and textures vary? They may go back to the stream they observed. What living creatures can they see? They may watch the sky. How is the weather different? What do the clouds look like?

- Nature journaling is a motivating homework assignment. Once students have experience observing, they can be encouraged to add to their nature journals whenever they want. They can use their nature collections throughout the school year to enhance the study of geometry, poetry writing, local geography, technical drawing, and of course, science themes related to biology, botany, earth science, and meteorology. At the end of the school year, the students will have a nature journal typical of a "real" scientist.

Assessment

Nature journals give teachers an opportunity to collect data and assess student understanding of concepts and the inquiry process. Teachers can use nature journals as both formative and summative assessments by looking at the use of cross-curricular skills, the asking and answering of meaningful questions, the understanding of big ideas, and the effective use of the inquiry process. Data trends quickly emerge. This data can then be used to inform instruction as well as provide an assessment measure required for the school district.

Student improvement in critical thinking and reflection comes after time and exposure to nature journals. Continued reference by the teacher to previously taught concepts increases the likelihood of the nature journal's endurance as a tool that the students will continue to use in and out of school.

CONCLUSION

Nature journals, as a learning tool, provide meaningful experiences necessary for authentic inquiry. They yield experiences that encourage reflection and the formulation of "big questions." Through the use of nature journals, students are able to become critical and creative thinkers, helping to build a learning community where authentic inquiry occurs through curriculum integration.

Teaching Memoir: There Are No Dumb Questions!

Robin D. Smith

"Honors British Literature . . . Mr. Hatch, Period C," I read from the schedule. I knew the class was one floor down and in the English wing, so I took my time getting to class among an obvious influx of scurrying, confused, and anxious-looking first- and second-year students. Confidence surged through my body; I had survived my sophomore year of high school—deemed to be perhaps the most difficult and rigorous year St. John's had to offer—and was excited about junior year. French III and physics went by swimmingly the first two periods.

As I made my way down the corridor—not even halfway through my schedule for the day—I was thinking about how easy it was going to be to make honor roll while playing basketball and completing the required service project.

Mild banter overran the room as the final bell rang. For many, the final bell was not a big enough indicator that class was ready to begin. *SLAM*. Mr. Hatch's foolproof class starter: the door. Some mild formalities such as attendance, a review of the course syllabus, and then it was off to the discussion on *Grendel*. Sure, the summer reading of *Grendel* was not one of my fondest memories, but anything was better than Honors English last year.

Or so I thought. As Mr. Hatch concluded our *Grendel* discussion, he made his way over to the window near his desk. He stared out of the window for a second and without warning began to speak in verse and in a language that none of us recognized. He picked up a large stack of papers on the window sill, walked to the student's desk nearest him, and with a nod instructed Brandon to start passing out the thick packets. I sat in one of the aisles farthest from the window and by the time my copy reached me, the confidence I had coming into class that morning quickly fizzled into anxiety.

I looked down at the first page. I squinted to make sure that I was seeing the text accurately. Mr. Hatch began to talk, revealing that we would be reading the poem upon which Grendel's character was based, *Beowulf.* Without further explanation, we were told to read silently for ten minutes. We all complied and attempted to read the poem, which had been translated from its original version into a newer form of "Old English."

After five minutes of trying to find some recognizable words in the text, my anxiety evolved into pure panic. If this English class wasn't even going to be in English, exactly what was I going to do? Looking at the facial expressions on my classmates, I did not feel alone. Everyone was absolutely sullen; many of us saw the honor roll becoming more and more unattainable.

Mr. Hatch asked us some questions about *Beowulf*; none of us answered. Who wants to be the "dumb" kid? Worse even, who wants to ask a dumb question? Entering our junior year of high school, my class had not yet learned the art of asking questions and getting clarification. We were stuck on the all-important façade of looking like we knew what we were doing, but all the while not having a blessed clue about what was going on.

Our first lesson in Mr. Hatch's class was not about the rhyme and meter of Old English poetry. Rather, he focused on the importance of asking questions, regardless of how "dumb" they might sound. Why didn't anyone ask for a more current version of the poem, he queried. He had copies available for anyone who wanted one!

Mr. Hatch continued to establish a culture in which it was okay to question things and okay to not know everything—something that had never been accepted in our previous classes. I cherished the reassurance I received from Mr. Hatch whenever I asked a "dumb" question. And yes, I made the honor roll.

Today, I still remember this lesson I learned from Mr. Hatch. As a result, I encourage questions of all kinds from my own students, regardless of how "dumb" they may seem. As a constructivist educator who wants to teach the way my students actually learn, I have come to regard the questions that my students ask as more valuable than the questions I pose to them. I am constantly reevaluating my methods and my curriculum and seeking ways to improve my teaching. Without "dumb" questions, this would be impossible!

Chapter Five

Teaching Social Studies: What Is the Right Answer?

Kathleen M. Doyle

Who has not suffered through a history class where every class period was spent copying the teacher's notes and memorizing seemingly random names and dates, while each evening was spent reading "the chapter" and answering "the questions"? Sometime between Socrates and 1900, teaching practices and beliefs about learning changed—for the worse.

Socrates invited learners to ponder life's essential questions. Today, students are fed "the answers" before they have even reflected upon the questions. It does not take long for them to conclude that their own questions must not be important. A constructivist approach in the classroom nourishes the hunger students have for answers to life's essential questions.

Far too many social studies programs are determined solely by a textbook—or worse—a state test. Socrates would be turning in his grave if he saw how state testing programs now decide what should be taught—and even how many minutes should be spent "teaching" each "right answer." It is no wonder that test scores are not increasing, drop-out rates remain high, and the average student is not engaged in learning.

Too often, history is taught as a set of facts and conclusions. Little room is left for "Why?" "How?" or even, "Who cares?" Is "In what year did the Civil War begin?" really one of life's—or history's—essential questions? There are many excellent reasons to study the Civil War. For example, a study of the Civil War can help students understand some of the reasons wars are fought—or even why the election of President Barack Obama was so historic. But memorizing the dates and names associated with the Civil War will not help a student understand why war happens, or why racism still exists (both of which *are* essential questions).

An understanding of chronology is important. Without a sense of chronology, students cannot make sense of history. Too often, however, chronology is the only lesson. One problem with teaching history as a long list of chronological names, dates, and facts is that the list just keeps getting longer. An even more significant problem is that these "list lessons" do not promote higher-level thinking skills.

Limited funds, resources, and time often make a textbook the main source of information in a social studies classroom. Textbooks can be valuable resources. They are usually well researched and attractively designed. An effective teacher knows how and when to use a textbook. Unfortunately, in addition to the lack of resources, a lack of training often leads many teachers to rely almost exclusively on the textbook to form the curriculum.

A textbook-driven curriculum implies that everything important can be found in one book—a book that by necessity can only devote limited space to important events, often reducing significant, historic controversies down to bland tidy conclusions such as "the dropping of the atomic bomb may have been necessary to end World War II." Fortunately, thanks to technology, more and more social studies teachers are able to supplement or even supplant the textbook.

A constructivist approach to teaching social studies embraces the historic controversies that have shaped the United States and world events for better and worse. Students in a constructivist classroom may still conclude that dropping the atomic bomb was necessary given the historic context and alternatives, but only after an in-depth study of the various arguments both for and against the dropping of the bomb and an in-depth look at the results of the decision—both short-term and long-term. This type of activity obviously requires a variety of sources.

Consider a traditional high school world history course syllabus, which typically promises to be a comprehensive study of world history to include prehistory, the first civilizations, early empires, ancient Greece and Rome, ancient China, African kingdoms, exploration—and the list continues all the way up to the twenty-first century. Such a syllabus suggests a course filled with names, dates, and events. Thousands of years of history (and economics, geography, and civics) cannot be learned in any meaningful way in 185 days.

Anyone who has ever taken or taught such a "comprehensive" course knows the frustration and pressure of trying to learn or teach so much information in so little time. The goal is often to cover as much information as possible, and the most efficient methods to achieve this goal are through lectures and readings. Many teachers who use this approach will admit that they hope that students *at least* learn how to take notes and manage their time so that they can be successful in college.

GETTING STARTED

A constructivist approach to teaching social studies demands a critical analysis of history's lessons and a trust that teachers (rather than test developers or textbook publishers) know their students and their subject matter. A school that wishes to add more depth to the curriculum might begin by having teachers share their opinions regarding the essential purpose of education.

Teachers can brainstorm their own individual content and skill lists, making sure they can answer why each item is essential. The teachers can then share their lists with other teachers and identify what they have in common. They could compare their lists to the five thousand items that E. D. Hirsch identified in his book *Cultural Literacy: What Every American Needs to Know* (1987). As they reach consensus (not a simple or quick process) on the essential knowledge and skills, they can begin to design their curriculum and take ownership of their work.

When teachers gather to brainstorm and debate what knowledge and skills are essential, their conversations eventually lead them to extract the essence of historical events. Does every single war need to be "studied" or might one or two case studies suffice? Why do we study wars in history? Many will insist that we study history so that it will not repeat itself. If that is truly the reason, what is the best approach for helping students to identify patterns of cause and effect? How does *telling* them the patterns give them analytical skills?

There are certainly learners who can digest what they are told and apply that information to new situations. The typical student is not that type of learner.

ESSENTIAL QUESTIONS

Compare the lecture/textbook-driven course to one that emphasizes a number of skills and an early grasp of and appreciation for essential questions—all of which will be beneficial in college. The questions are those that people throughout the ages have asked. Students have the same questions:

- Where did we come from? How do we know? What do we know? What don't we know?
- How do/did people use religion to make sense of their world? When/how does religion lead to conflict? What is/has been the nature of the relationship between religion and government?
- How do we know what is true? What is the truth?

- What is the common good? How can the common good be cared for? Can utopia exist?
- How can peace and security be maintained?

CONSTRUCTIVIST METHODS AND ACTIVITIES

In a constructivist classroom, the teacher does not *give* his or her answers to these questions, expecting the students to obediently copy notes and then memorize the notes long enough to give these notes back on a test. Instead, the teacher creates a comfortable environment for the discussion and exploration of such essential questions, offers and allows choices, manages time, and assesses understanding utilizing a variety of evaluation tools.

Students in a constructivist classroom might

- explore creation stories, look at the controversies surrounding evolution versus creationism, put John Scopes and Galileo on trial;
- perform a skit on the day in the life of a follower of one of the world religions;
- debate the impact of violence in the media;
- research individuals such as Plato, Karl Marx, and Ralph Nader and identify their utopian visions;
- debate the role of technology in creating the "good life";
- analyze America's founding as a utopia.

CRITICISMS AND MISCONCEPTIONS

Many people are uncomfortable with this approach. Everyone has their own cultural literacy list. Colleagues and parents and even students will want to know why "such and such" isn't being taught and "shouldn't students at least *be exposed* to this information so that they can say, 'I've heard of that'?" From a constructivist viewpoint, mere exposure is not a worthwhile way to spend the valuable and limited time students and teachers have together. How is mere exposure to many bits of information better than an in-depth study of a critical issue or question? "I understand that" is far more meaningful than "I've heard of that."

Why is it that in college, a student can spend an entire semester studying about the Great Depression, but in high school, one week is deemed adequate? Such an approach is not compatible with an adolescent's development. Mere exposure cannot create enthusiastic learners.

We want students to really understand, don't we? We want citizens who can be critical consumers of information, don't we? Delivering predigested conclusions has the opposite effect. For example, how can a citizen grasp the complexities of the perennial immigration debate if his or her classroom experience with this important issue came from a fact-filled historical lecture or chapter in a textbook? The lecture or textbook typically has distilled the rich, long history of immigration into what the teacher or editor considers to be the essential facts. Essential facts should not be confused with essential questions.

Constructivism is often wrongfully criticized as relativism—the idea that whatever knowledge and skills the child chooses to learn is "the right answer." Constructivism does not consist of assigning a big project and then stepping back to watch what the children decide to do with it. The teacher is still responsible for guiding, challenging, and identifying certain outcomes—and in history, those outcomes typically involve a variety of perspectives—not neat, tidy, absolutist answers. Therein lies the challenge for good constructivist teaching and real constructivist learning.

AN EXAMPLE

A constructivist approach to a unit on immigration might begin by asking the students their opinion on some current immigration legislation. For the past century or so, the questions have always been, "Who should be allowed into America?" and "How do we do this fairly?" More recent questions might include, "Should a fence be built between Mexico and the United States to keep illegal immigrants from Latin America from crossing the border?" "If the police find an illegal immigrant working in a factory, who should get in trouble—the immigrant or the employer?"

The teacher might begin the unit by asking students to write what they already know about the topic and what questions they have. Students can also write their own answers to questions such as those listed above. The teacher can collect the students' written responses and identify the gaps in knowledge and the inaccurate information that invariably turns up. Alternatively, the teacher can invite and manage a class-wide discussion. (Managing discussions of controversial issues takes practice, but it is well worth the effort.)

When the teacher allows time for reflection and discussion, students often have their own questions, which invariably match the essential questions the teachers had arrived at in their own brainstorming sessions. A teacher might be tempted to save time and "give" the questions, but that undermines the students' opportunity to begin constructing his or her own knowledge.

A debate is an effective method for learning in a constructivist classroom. Debates offer excellent opportunities for research, public speaking, critical thinking, listening, and learning content. The teacher can distribute current articles that give various perspectives, and invite the students to find their own articles (a tremendous opportunity to help students to become critical consumers of information, especially since students will often initially bring in "Google garbage").

As a result of their research and the debate, students will see that immigration policy is truly complex and they will learn some important historical, cultural, geographic, economic, and civics lessons as well. They will leave this project fully appreciating why immigration is such an important chapter in U.S. history.

Preparing for a debate takes time. Spending a couple of weeks on a project may seem like an impossible luxury in the current test-anxious climate. Research and reflection take time. However, the depth of research and reflection typically promotes enthusiasm and elicits many questions on the part of the students. After such a debate, they want to know the history. They want the specifics and they have the skills to seek out the various, often conflicting answers. There is no need to force-feed this content. The students are hungry for more knowledge. See this chapter's appendixes for an example of a debate lesson.

There are many other tools besides debates that can be used in a constructivist classroom, such as mock trials, skits (written and performed by the students), research papers, interviews, persuasive essays, creative-writing opportunities, and the list goes on. The occasional presentation of information (lecture) along with assigned readings is also appropriate. A variety in approach and assessment keeps the students engaged and provides opportunities for success for all learning styles.

CONCLUSION

Identifying essential questions to guide methods and assessment results in a rich, deeper, more effective education for all students than the traditional reliance on chapters in a textbook or preparation for a state test. There simply are no neat, tidy, absolute answers for life's (and history's) essential questions. Life's big questions are big because there are no simple answers. To teach as if there are simple answers is the wrong answer.

APPENDIX A: THE DREAM ACT DEBATE

Proposition: The Dream Act Should Become Law

About the Dream Act (acronym for Development, Relief, and Education of Alien Minors Act): The act is geared toward young people who (illegally) entered the United States before the age of sixteen, have lived here for at least five years, have graduated from a U.S. high school or received a GED, and are of good moral character. They would apply and complete six years of work to include college and/or two years in the military in order to become a legal U.S. citizen.

Your tasks:

- Find at least two articles that (affirm) support the Dream Act becoming law (or that are sympathetic to young illegal immigrants or that are in some way sympathetic to all illegal immigrants). Print the articles and bring them to class. 10 pts.
- Find two articles that (negate) oppose all of the above listed in #1. Print and bring to class. 10 pts. *Remember the rules about finding valid, reliable articles!*
- Develop *two* arguments that affirm (support) the proposition.
- Develop *two* arguments that negate (oppose) the proposition.
- Use Noodletools to develop your works cited page.

= 100 pts.

- Participate in the actual debate. (Exemplary participation means that you participate several times with actual research.)

= 50 pts.

(If you are absent, you will make up these 50 pts. with a persuasive essay.)

APPENDIX B: WRITTEN DEBATE ARGUMENTS CHECKLIST

This rubric is used by students to plan their debate and then used again by the teacher as an assessment at the end of the activity.

Criteria	Arg. 1	Arg. 2	Arg. 3	Arg. 4
The proposition is worded properly at the top of each argument. (The proposition does not change.) 2 pts. each				
The argument is accurately identified as "affirmative" or "negative" (affirmative supports the proposition, negative refutes the proposition). The argument is clear and concise—and more specific than the proposition. The argument is not identical to any other argument. 4 pts. each				
Evidence #1 gives actual proof for your argument, is clear, is explained in *your* own words, except for short quotations that simply cannot be worded more clearly by you. 4 pts. each				
The source for your information in evidence #1 is cited— usually by identifying the author and paragraph number (or page number). If author is not known, include article title. A web address alone is inadequate. 3 pts. each				
Evidence #2—More proof to support the argument. Different from evidence #1. Same criteria. 4 pts. each				
Source for evidence #2 is cited. Must come from a different source than evidence #1. 3 pts. each				
Conclusion clearly summarizes the points made by your evidence, is consistent with your argument, and does not introduce new information. 2 pts. each				
Works cited page lists all the source information for any work that you cited in your evidence. Alphabetical order by author—or title if no author. Works cited page does not cite sources by using only a web address. 12 pts. total				

APPENDIX C: WRITTEN DEBATE ARGUMENTS ASSESSMENT RUBRIC

Scoring Key: 1=Unacceptable, 2=Limited, 3=Acceptable, 4=Exceptional

	4	3	2	1
Proposition	Is phrased accurately at the top of each argument	Is phrased accurately but missing from some of the arguments	Is not phrased accurately in places	Is missing
Argument	Each argument is strong, clear, concise, accurately identified as affirmative or negative, in your own words	Most of the arguments are reasonably strong and clear, in your own words, might not be labeled properly as affirmative/negative	One or two of the arguments are not your own words, or too wordy or too vague or weak	Your arguments are not in complete sentences and therefore are not arguments
Evidence #1 and #2	Clearly and adequately supports or proves the argument; is explained in *your* own words, except for short quotations that simply cannot be worded more clearly by you *and* each evidence comes from a different source.	Somewhat supports/proves the argument—or is good evidence, but for a different argument; parts of the quote could have been put into your own words; *and* each evidence comes from a source different from evidence #1	Evidence does not convincingly prove/support the argument or is not written as clearly as it could be; both pieces of evidence come from the same source	Evidence is not relevant to the argument or is missing
Citations for Evidence #1 and #2	Accurately cited from a valid, reliable source; citation appears on works cited page	Format is inaccurate, or source is questionable, but citation appears on works cited page	Citation does not appear on works cited page	Citation is missing
Conclusion	Conclusion clearly summarizes points, is consistent with argument, does not introduce new information, is not identical to the argument	Most conclusions are mostly clear and consistent with arguments, do not introduce new information, are not identical to the arguments	Some conclusions introduce new information or are identical to the arguments	Missing
Works Cited Page	Accurate format, includes only works that were cited in the evidence	Format is mostly accurate and includes only works that were cited in the evidence	Includes works that were not cited in the evidence and/or is missing works that were cited in the evidence	Missing

APPENDIX D: DEBATE PARTICIPATION RUBRIC
SELF-ASSESSMENT

Circle or highlight *each* point that best describes your performance.

Understanding of Topic	I completely understood the information we discussed.	I think I understood most of what we discussed. I could have given better examples. I gave some evidence, but could have given more. I understood most, but not all of the "technical" words.	I'm not sure I understood the info we were discussing. I wasn't sure which examples of info to use to make my points. I am not sure my information is correct. I didn't understand most of the "technical" words.
Contribution and Group Dynamics	I helped make sure the discussion stayed on topic. I knew just what info was needed to contribute to the discussion. I did not interrupt; I was polite. When I disagree with someone, I know how to do it so that I don't hurt anyone's feelings.	I participated in the group when asked to by others, but I usually don't unless I am asked. I generally listened to others, but I occasionally got distracted. I sometimes interrupted. I tried not to hurt others' feelings, but I think I sometimes did.	I usually don't follow what is going on. I talked too much. I didn't talk at all. I don't know how to "argue" and still be polite. I don't think it is important for everyone to have a chance to talk
Use of Language	I tried to say things in a way that the group would understand. I didn't use more words than I needed to.	I think I sometimes used more words than needed to make a point. I think I sometimes used words that others didn't understand.	I'm not sure how to say things in ways others will understand. I sometimes don't pay attention to how I say things.
Strength of Arguments	I think my arguments were strong, convincing, and supported by relevant evidence.	Most of the times that I spoke my arguments were convincing and my evidence was relevant.	I felt that my arguments were not convincing and that I didn't have strong evidence.

The results of this rubric may be used to develop personal or group goals for the next debate.

A Sample Argument

Proposition: School uniforms improve the overall atmosphere in a school.
Affirmative argument #1: School uniforms improve student behavior.

Evidence #1:

Many teachers and administrators perceive improved behavior when students wear uniforms. Principal Rudolph Saunders of Stephen Decatur Middle School in Clinton, Maryland, states that students simply behave better when they are dressed in uniforms. "It's like night and day. We have 'dress down' days, and the kids' behavior is just completely different on those days." He also perceives that students fight less and they focus on their schoolwork more. Teacher Betty Mikesell-Bailey, from the same school, says that in-school suspensions have declined and test scores have gone up since they instituted uniforms. Students no longer bully one another over their clothing (Viadero, 2005, pp. 1–2).

Evidence #2:

Long Beach, California, was one of the first big-city school districts to adopt uniforms in 1994. Within the first year, crime dropped 22 percent. Schools in and around St. Louis began adopting uniforms in 2000, and according to Superintendent Jed Deets of the Cahokia School District, behavior has improved. He suggests that the evidence is clear on "dress-down days" when he sees "a marked increase in behavior problems" (Aguilar, 2005, p. 1).

Conclusion: Uniforms clearly have a positive impact on discipline in schools.

REFERENCES

Aguilar, A. (2005). Belleville West High sizes up uniform policy. *St. Louis Post Dispatch*. April.

Hirsch, E. D., Jr. (1987). *Cultural literacy: What every American needs to know*. Boston: Houghton Mifflin.

Viadero, D. (2005). Uniform effects. *Education Week*. April.

Teaching Memoir: Sam

Jill E. Cole

Sam came to second grade that warm September day with too-big jeans, a backpack without lunch, and a frown on his face. He had just begun living with a new foster family and was entering the fifth school he had attended in his troubled seven years.

"I *don't* read," Sam told me when I said he could choose a book from the classroom library.

"He needs to be tested," said the school psychologist after reading Sam's file.

"He should be labeled for special education," recommended the county director of special services after scoring the test.

"No," I said. "Give him . . . give *us* some time."

I brought Sam close to me as I read aloud to the class so he could see the illustrations and watch me as I tracked the print. I surreptitiously left books on his desk that I thought he would like. I listened to his stories and wrote them down on brightly colored paper for Sam to read and illustrate. And I waited.

One day Sam came to me with a book.

"There's a funny dog on the front," he said.

"The title is *Hot Dog* by Molly Coxe. Would you like me to read it to you?" I asked.

Sam didn't answer, so I read the book once and then again to make comments on the illustrations and point to the words. Sam took the book back to his desk and flipped through it several times. Then he went page by page, pointing to the words just as I had done. One by one. Slow and steady. He giggled twice.

Later that day, Sam told me, "I read that book. It's funny."

"Wonderful," I smiled.

"Want to hear?"

I squelched a "hallelujah" and nodded sedately instead.

Each page in the book had a short sentence that told the story of a "hot" dog on a summer day who finally convinces a little girl to sprinkle him with the garden hose. He is now a "chilly" dog. Sam and I laughed together.

Sam read that book many times over the next week—to me, to a friend, silently to himself. In fact, he continued to read the book almost daily for the rest of the school year.

But he also read other books. Funny books, animal books, short books, long books.

One day in December, Sam called me to his desk to show me his new favorite book. "I *love* this book," he said.

I asked a colleague to watch the class briefly so I could step out into the hallway to weep.

Later in the day, during a reading circle, I asked Sam if he would like to read the book for his classmates. His expression and a shake of the head said no, but I said, "You are ready, Sam. You can do it."

Sam showed the cover to his classmates and began to read. He didn't stop until the end of the book when everyone clapped. Sam looked at me and said, "I *can* read!"

In January, the test displayed higher scores and the county director of special services crossed Sam's name off the special education list, although he still recommended that Sam repeat second grade.

In April, the test declared that Sam was reading on a third-grade level and had scored almost as high in math. He was ready to move on.

On the last day of school, Sam was taken away by social workers to yet another foster home. And although I never saw him again, *Hot Dog* is a permanent part of my classroom library. Now I read it every semester to my teacher candidates with a story of what it sometimes takes to change a child's experience in the classroom—a firm "no," a little patience, and a funny book.

REFERENCE

Coxe, M. (1998). *Hot dog.* New York: Random House.

Chapter Six

Motivating Students to Read Using Constructivist Strategies

Jill E. Cole

Reading instruction has certainly been in the limelight lately, and in many ways, I rejoice. Additional funding is being provided for reading instruction, schools are focused on improving the reading achievement of their students, and legislators have reading instruction on the tips of their tongues. In other ways, however, I lament. Scripted reading programs are proliferating, some money is still not going to the right places, and teachers are losing the trust and respect of the public while standardized tests are gaining it.

So, my task is clear. Students need to become successful, lifelong readers, and teachers need tools to impel this transformation. How can I accomplish this while taking advantage of the benefits of the current educational climate, while minimizing the problems? The answer lies within the philosophies and practices of motivation and constructivism.

INTRINSIC AND EXTRINSIC MOTIVATION

First, the definition of motivation, as it will be used in this chapter, needs to be clearly stated. Intrinsic motivation involves "the forces within an organism that arouse and direct behavior" (Harris & Hodges, 1995, p. 158). Malouf (1983) describes intrinsic motivation as a return to a particular behavior without external pressure to do so, even when other options are available. For classroom use, perhaps Oldfather and Dahl (1994, p. 141) explain it best as a "continuing impulse to learn." When students are intrinsically motivated to learn, they engage in a task for its own sake. Intrinsic motivation promotes long-term learning and lasting change.

Extrinsic motivation is characterized by the use of external rewards such as grades, prizes, stickers, and even praise. Extrinsic motivators result in short-term learning, and when students expect rewards, motivation often decreases (Kohn, 1996). In fact, Kohn places reward and punishment in the same category and states that both are coercive and manipulative. Students who are motivated extrinsically engage in a task solely to receive a reward or incentive or to avoid punishment. This may force students to be compliant in our classrooms, but it does not support them in the important journey of learning.

Intrinsic motivation to read should be the benchmark. It is students who are motivated intrinsically who will read voraciously and critically, master the skills and strategies needed for successful academic achievement, as well as assume a lifelong stance as a reader.

For the purposes of this chapter, the terms "motivation" and "intrinsic motivation" are used interchangeably.

MOTIVATION TO READ AND LEARN

The National Reading Panel (National Institute of Child Health and Human Development, 2000) identified five areas of reading instruction for purposes of analysis: phonemic awareness, phonics, fluency, vocabulary, and comprehension. All five are crucial to providing effective instruction for students to become successful, strategic readers. However, while carefully planned instruction in reading skills and strategies is important, it is incomplete (Morrow, 2002), and the missing piece is student motivation to read and learn.

Developing skillful readers is not enough. In fact, the National Reading Panel (NRP) stated that although motivational factors were not considered in the report, it did not mean that such factors were insignificant or unproductive. We need readers who are motivated to be strategic, purposeful, self-directed, and lifelong.

Time constraints are often an excuse for not including motivational activities into the curriculum. However, the motivating of students does not take the place of research-based instruction, nor does it necessarily fill time that could be better used by providing that instruction. Motivation clarifies and strengthens the cognitive processes of reading and learning to read and fits into the curriculum *during* instruction. After all, children (and all human beings) don't really learn anything without being motivated to do so (Smith, 1997).

In education right now, we are firmly fixed in an environment that supports an organized structure of assessment and standardized testing. We want our students to perform well on the required tests so they are prepared for future instruction and assessment, and we *need* them to perform well to preserve jobs, schools, and the education system as we know it. So why would we *not* make certain that our students were accomplished, motivated readers?

Motivation to read can assist them to achieve well on the tests. It is, in fact, crucial that students do not lose motivation; if they do, they most likely will *not* do well on the tests. Pressley, Dolezal, Raphael, Mohan, Roehrig, and Bogner (2003) studied primary grade classrooms and found that motivational teachers enabled their students to perform better on standardized tests than nonmotivational teachers.

Calkins (2001) looks at the issue from another side. What if, in the effort to increase student achievement and raise test scores, we are actually engendering student disengagement and apathy in the classroom? A focus on tests and test preparation can push aside classroom events that support student interests, self-selected reading, and significant time to read. In the effort to increase literacy, we may actually be advancing aliteracy. Aliterate students may read when absolutely required to do so, but would not choose to read for personal reasons, to increase knowledge, or to participate in society.

In their long-term research, Pressley and colleagues (2003) found a variety of "motivational mechanisms" that triggered intrinsic motivation in students, especially when it seemed motivation had already declined. Some of them are the following:

- Teacher modeling interest
- Sincere praise
- Collaborative learning
- Student success
- Teacher caring
- Using students' interests
- Giving choices
- Decreasing rewards
- Meaningful work
- Allowing autonomy
- Appropriate challenge
- Informative, not judgmental, feedback

Focusing on the intrinsic motivation mechanisms listed above has many benefits that can aid teachers in promoting classroom participation, engagement, and learning. Pressley and colleagues (2003) also compiled the following list of benefits of motivated behavior that they documented in elementary students. These dispositions would certainly allow teachers to better prepare their students to successfully complete classroom assignments and assessments of all types.

- On-task behavior
- Participation in class
- Thoughtfulness in responses
- Interest and excitement
- Deep thinking
- Making connections
- Authentic consideration of the information presented by the teacher
- Emotional involvement in the content
- Prevention of management problems

In short, Pressley and colleagues (2003, p. 163) summarize by stating that "an insight we have had as we have completed this work is that by focusing on motivation, everything else follows." Berger (2003) adds that once a student experiences success in the school culture, which intrinsic motivators can provide, he or she is never the same. The student moves from reading text to being a reader; from asking, "How much of this do I have to know?" to "I can't get enough of this." An important avenue for creating this kind of change is through constructivist practices in the classroom.

CONSTRUCTIVIST PRACTICE

Constructivism is defined as a philosophical paradigm that posits that human beings learn by constructing new knowledge through connections to current knowledge structures and experiences (Wadsworth, 2004). The focus is on the learning. True teaching occurs when learner events are planned according to *how* students learn, not simply to complete the five workbook pages for the day.

In general, teachers who hold a constructivist philosophy create learning environments that allow children to discover connections, ask questions, take risks in learning without penalty, participate in activities with relevance to their lives, receive developmentally appropriate instruction, feel part of the learning community, and, ultimately, construct meaning. Teachers, then, seek student perceptions before teaching, adapt the curriculum to meet their needs, and assess to inform future instruction. When students are taught the way that they learn, the very act of learning is intrinsically motivating.

Learning is not linear, much as we would like it to be. The traditional approach to teaching has involved the teacher presenting content to the students, the students taking notes or writing a paper or participating in a discussion, and then taking a test to demonstrate learning. At best, this sends the content to the short-term memory, where it is mostly forgotten the week after the test.

Smith (1997) equates long-term memory with learning; it is there forever. However, in order to get the content there "forever," there must be a structure to help students connect this new learning with prior knowledge so they construct new meaning and it makes sense. When students (or any human beings) are constructing meaning and it is making sense to them, motivation is intrinsic and automatic. The learning is enjoyable, even if it is challenging and takes effort.

Human beings of all ages learn continuously and effortlessly throughout life when connections are being made and the information makes sense. When the constructivist philosophy is carried out in the classroom, appropriate structures are put in place that help students tap into prior knowledge, make connections, and construct personal meaning.

One of the features of this chapter is to present practical examples of the potency of constructivist methods of teaching that allow students to construct new meaning and experience intrinsic motivation as they learn phonemic awareness, phonics, fluency, vocabulary, and comprehension.

Our "default drive" as teachers should be to select appropriate content, consider how to motivate students intrinsically, and teach the way students learn. For each lesson, the questions that should be asked are: What is the important content I need to teach? How am I going to motivate my students to learn it? What teaching strategies will accomplish this? A collection of learner events follows that demonstrates the fusion of intentional intrinsic motivation to learn with best-practice constructivist teaching.

LEARNER EVENT—PHONEMIC AWARENESS

Phonemic awareness is the ability of a child to deliberately identify and manipulate the sounds of language, such as phonemes, onsets, rimes, and syllables (McGee & Richgels, 2008). Being phonemically aware is a vital skill for young children to hold in order for reading instruction to be meaningful and successful, and motivation is an essential component to ensure its mastery.

For children who have a background of being read to and participating in frequent and meaningful conversations at home, phonemic awareness may be automatic by the time they reach school. However, many children are not phonemically aware in kindergarten and first grade, and need explicit instruction. This presents one of the conundrums of teaching: some children already know the information, and others do not. For phonemic awareness, this is an easy fix. The best way to develop phonemic awareness is to "play" with words and sounds.

William Glasser (1998) reminds us that "fun" is one of the five basic human needs along with safety, belonging, power, and freedom. The constructivist instructional model that follows uses "fun" to intrinsically motivate students to learn.

Picture This in the Classroom . . .

Mr. Baker begins the lesson by introducing a new picture book to his kindergarteners. He has chosen *The Magic Hat* (2002), by Mem Fox and illustrated by Tricia Tusa, which has rhyming text. As he reads aloud, he emphasizes the rhyming words with his voice. When the book is completed, Mr. Baker asks the class what they noticed about the book. The conversation may include many things that the students have noticed; however, someone will eventually mention the rhyming words.

"What are rhyming words?" asks Mr. Baker. "How can you tell when words rhyme?" He lets the children answer and discuss and then says, "Today we're going to learn more about rhyming words. Listen carefully as I read some words from the book we just read."

"Hat and that. Do these words rhyme? Why?" Mr. Baker guides students to talk about the "at" sounds they hear in both words.

"Road—toad. Balloon—baboon." The children laugh at the words and discussion continues that focuses on specifically what makes these pairs of words rhyme. Mr. Baker tries another pair of words from the book.

"Magic—move. Do these words rhyme?" To some cries of "No!" Mr. Baker asks all the children to think to themselves about why these two words do not rhyme. He repeats them a few times and then elicits a conversation that points out that although the two words begin the same, they do not end with the same sounds.

"How about hairy—head, spun—stare?"

The conversation for each pair of words focuses on why the words do not rhyme. Then Mr. Baker mixes them up. "Hop—stop, wink—think, bear—kangaroo." The class then comes up with a definition of rhyming words together. Mr. Baker records the definition, using the students' wording, so he can use it again when the class moves from recognizing rhymes by sound to reading them in text (such as "rhyming words end with the same sounds").

To close the lesson, Mr. Baker asks the class if they would like to hear the book again or if they would like to choose another book with rhyming text (he has *Chicka Chicka Boom Boom* [1989] by Bill Martin Jr. and John Archambault, illustrated by Lois Ehlert, ready in case). Unanimously they decide to have Mr. Baker reread *The Magic Hat*. Mr. Baker then puts the book in the classroom library so students can pick it up on their own during free reading time.

This lesson not only asks students to recognize rhyming words but helps them define the concept for themselves—constructing new knowledge. This aids in long-term retention, especially when the definition and further examples and nonexamples continue to be used in the classroom. Intrinsic motivation is addressed by using a piece of children's literature that was chosen specifically by Mr. Baker because he thought his students would enjoy it. And he was right, although he had another choice ready if the students desired a change.

When planning this lesson, Mr. Baker asked himself the three questions mentioned earlier:

- What is the important content I need to teach? (phonemic awareness—recognizing and defining rhyming words)
- How am I going to motivate my students to learn it? (interesting literature and words, the meaningful work of creating a definition together that will continue to be used in the classroom, choice in the closing book)
- What teaching strategies will accomplish this? (comparing examples and nonexamples of rhyming words, posting a student-generated definition).

And because of his attention to planning, Mr. Baker's class exhibited several positive learning dispositions (Pressley et al., 2003) such as on-task behavior, participation in class, interest and excitement, and authentic consideration of the information presented by the teacher.

LEARNER EVENT—PHONICS

Lenski and Nierstheimer (2004, p. 178) define phonics as "the knowledge of the relationships between letters and sounds and the ability to combine or blend those sounds represented by letters into words." When students connect the marks on the page of a book with the letter sounds they know, they are using phonics. Phonics is a tool that helps children decode words in order to access meaning. Most good readers understand and use phonics, but phonics itself is not the end result; successful reading is.

The NRP (National Institute of Child Health and Human Development, 2000) decidedly calls for systematic, explicit phonics instruction to be coupled with motivation in order to create independent readers. Independent readers are those who *can* read and also *choose* to read. Research tells us that struggling readers simply don't read as much as independent readers and programs designed to assist struggling readers often focus on phonics skills in isolation so readers read text even less. This is self-defeating. Phonics lessons need to relate directly to text that is meaningful for students.

The next lesson also demonstrates constructivist instruction by using examples and nonexamples of phonic patterns. Time is spent exploring the patterns in isolation to ensure understanding, but students are then immediately connected to real text that they can read and enjoy. The lesson begins with a word sort highlighting short and long a sounds in common words. Word sorts can be taught whole class or in small, flexible groups. Regardless of reading achievement, students can benefit from working with word sorts of various difficulty levels to learn patterns, word families, spelling, and phonics rules.

The example presented here is taught in a small group.

Picture This in the Classroom . . .

First-grade teacher Ms. Estevez introduces and reads aloud the picture book *Ira Sleeps Over* by Bernard Waber (1972) to her group of struggling readers. Ms. Estevez has deliberately chosen a book she thinks will engage her students and so the discussion after the reading is lively. The book also includes an assortment of words with short and long "a" sounds, which is the focus of today's lesson.

Ms. Estevez hands each student a set of fifteen word cards:

had	*take*	*hate*	*afternoon*
plan	*have*	*magic*	*glass*
that	*ask*	*name*	*stamp*
match	*change*	*late*	

The students spread their cards out in front of them and Ms. Estevez encourages them to sort the words into categories of their choice. She wants them to focus on the letters and patterns in the words, and all categories are considered correct as long as the child can explain why they came up with that category. Ms. Estevez has a sheet where she records the categories they create and their explanations so she can keep track of their thinking about words over time.

"What categories did you find?" Ms. Estevez asks.

"Had, have, and hate all start with *h*. Match and magic start with *m*."

"I made a sentence—Plan that magic!"

"I put match, stamp, and glass together because they are things you can see. Maybe I'll put in afternoon, too."

"Hate and late rhyme." Ms. Estevez is especially pleased when a student notices rhyming words because the class had worked with some rhyming words on the previous day.

"You have all done a wonderful job. You explained your categories so they make sense to me," says Ms. Estevez. "Let me give you two key words now. Find the words 'take' and 'had' and put them on the table. Let's say those words together. What does the 'a' sound like in each word? Can you find other words that have the same 'a' sound as 'had'? Please put those words under 'had.' Any words that have the same 'a' sound as 'take,' please put under 'take.'"

Ms. Estevez watches and listens as the students complete the sort. She helps when necessary and records what the children are doing.

"I see everyone is done. What do you notice about your words?"

"I have nine words under 'had' and only four under 'take.'"

"All the words under 'had' have an 'a' sound." (The student says the short "a" sound.)

"Yes!" says Ms. Estevez. "That is the short 'a' sound. Let's read those words again and everyone stretch out the a sound." Ms. Estevez notices some students include "have" and others do not, but she continues for now.

Another student responds, "All the words under 'take' have an 'a' [long 'a'] sound."

"Yes, again! Let's read those words stretching out the long 'a' sound. What else do you notice about these words?"

"All the words under 'take' start with different letters, but they end with 'e.'"

Ms. Estevez says, "That's an interesting point. They all end in 'e.' Let's reread all the words under 'had' and 'take.'" The students read the words together, and "have" is included in both lists. "Uh oh. Something strange is happening with 'have.' What do you think is going on?"

"It's an oddball!" several of the children chorus together.

"Yes," says Ms. Estevez. "We've talked before how English can be crazy sometimes. Will someone explain our word sort categories for today?"

Several children attempt summarizing statements and the class decides on, "Some words like 'had' have a short 'a' sound in them, and some words like 'bake' have a long 'a' sound. 'Have' is an oddball because it has a short 'a' sound, but it has an 'e' at the end, too."

"Nice explanation. What did all the long 'a' words have in common?"

"'E' at the end."

"Yes, we see that pattern. How does that help us?"

"When you see an 'a' in the middle of the word and an 'e' at the end, the 'a' sound will be like this—'a' [long 'a' sound]."

"Except for 'have'!"

"That's right. We have a pattern here, but as we've said before, patterns can have oddballs like 'have.' But 'have' is an important word. We use it a lot. Look around the room. Can you see the word 'have' on any of our posters or bulletin boards?" The children find some examples.

Ms. Estevez returns to the read-aloud from the beginning of the lesson. She wants to place the skill of long and short 'a' sounds back into the context of real reading. "Let's read the book again. Raise one hand if you hear a word with a short 'a' sound and two hands if you hear a word with a long 'a' sound."

"What about if we hear 'have'?"

"Good question. What would you like to do?"

"That's a short 'a' so we should raise just one hand."

"But we could wiggle the hand since it's a crazy oddball."

"Let's do that," says Ms. Estevez.

After the read-aloud, Ms. Estevez reviews the short and long 'a' sounds one more time before students return to their seats.

Ms. Estevez practiced the short and long "a" sounds with her students but encouraged them to use their own thinking to describe and explain the patterns and the "oddball." Students had the chance go further than being told the sounds of short and long "a" and memorizing some words that fit the pattern. The students sorted, took risks, and came up with unimportant information as well as the information needed for the concept.

Ms. Estevez helped them sort through their thinking, guiding them to the information they needed by connecting it to their current perceptions. She expressed sincere praise coupled with informative feedback (e.g., "You have all done a wonderful job. You explained your categories so they make sense to me").

Like Mr. Baker, Ms. Estevez also asked herself three questions as she planned:

- What is the important content I need to teach? (Words with short and long a patterns)
- How am I going to motivate my students to learn it? (Focusing on student success through taking risks, accepting and caring about the categories the students made, using sincere praise, and creating connections to meaningful work)
- What teaching strategy will accomplish this? (A word sort that would allow students to not only *practice* the skill but *understand* it as well)

Ms. Estevez was rewarded with on-task behavior, participation, interest, and deep thinking (Pressley et al., 2003).

LEARNER EVENT—VOCABULARY

Effective vocabulary instruction ensures that students actually remember and use the words that are taught to them. The purpose of teaching vocabulary is to increase students' ease and capabilities in reading and writing. Memorization does not accomplish this. Words that are tested on Friday are often forgotten by Monday and are rarely ever used in speech or in writing.

Sometimes it helps to rename vocabulary instruction to focus in on the true intent of the activity. "Word study" seems to point to a variety of possible pursuits that impact reading and writing, many of which are natural partners with motivation. Some examples include word sorts and hunts, graphic organizers, word histories, collections of interesting words, and the use of unique words in an assortment of reading and writing ventures.

One of the themes the fifth-grade studies is diversity. They look at diversity in many contexts, such as diversity in people, the environment, literature, mathematics, and countries around the world. In this next lesson, Mrs. Cho helps her fifth graders understand the diversity that exists in the English language.

Picture This in the Classroom . . .

Mrs. Cho puts the following words on the board:

tortilla	*dachshund*	*adobe*	*petite*	*a la mode*
ciao	*Kwanzaa*	*safari*	*kung fu*	*café au lait*
pizza	*espresso*	*geisha*	*gung ho*	*Feng Shui*
déjà vu	*sputnik*	*sauerkraut*	*burrito*	*kindergarten*

"What do you notice about these words?" asks Mrs. Cho. She gives the students time to think individually, then asks them to turn to the person next to them and share their ideas in pairs. After a few moments, Mrs. Cho begins a whole-class discussion.

"What do you think?" asks Mrs. Cho.

"They are words from other countries, I think, but I'm not sure about 'safari.'"

"They're words we use all the time, though."

"They're in our English dictionary. I looked some of them up."

"Can someone describe what these words have in common?" asks Mrs. Cho.

"They are words from other countires that we use in English."

"Yes, exactly. They are sometimes called loan words—words that have been loaned to us from other languages. Let's do some grouping. With your partner, make categories with these words using the language name. For example, make a category of Spanish words. What other languages do you see?"

Mrs. Cho lets the pairs work while she walks around and observes. Then she asks pairs of students to combine to make groups of four and compare their categories.

"Now let's put the categories on the board," says Mrs. Cho.

After some discussion and adjustments, the categories look like this:

Spanish	*French*	*Chinese*	*German*	*Italian*
tortilla	*petite*	*Kung fu*	*kindergarten*	*pizza*
burrito	*déjà vu*	*Feng Shui*	*dachshund*	*ciao*
adobe	*café au lait*	*gung ho*	*sauerkraut*	*espresso*
	a la mode	*geisha*		

African	*Russian*
Kwanzaa	*sputnik*
safari	

"What can you say about these categories?" asks Mrs. Cho. "What do they mean?"

"There were words from a lot of languages."

"We have lots of words in English that come from other languages."

"Yes, we do," says Mrs. Cho. "Why is this important?"

"Knowing that many words come from other languages gives us clues about spelling."

"Yeah, and pronunciation."

"It makes our language hard, but it makes it interesting, too."

"Those are all very good thoughts," says Mrs. Cho. "English is a diverse language. Our English language isn't just made up of English words. I find this somewhat surprising and very interesting."

"Just like America is a melting pot of nationalities and cultures, our language is a melting pot as well."

"What a good way to express it!" says Mrs. Cho. "Let's see what else we can discover about our diverse language. I'm going to send everyone on a word hunt. I want you to look for words you think come from other languages but are used often in English. You may look through books, posters, signs around the school, the Internet, and so on. Look everywhere you can think of and make a list of the words you find. I think your lists are going to tell us so much."

The students begin hunting and come back with long lists of words.

"It looks like everyone has lengthy lists. Wonderful!" says Mrs. Cho. "Tomorrow you will get into groups and share your lists. You'll be able to use our collection of dictionaries and other resources to determine the original languages of your words and pin down their meanings. Questions to think about are: How many languages do you think are represented in the English language? How do you think this happened? Why?

Also, if you see any other words at home that could go on your list, please add them. See everyone tomorrow!"

Throughout the word study and word hunt, the students made thoughtful responses to the activity making the connection between diversity and language. No management issues arose during the word hunt because students were used to activities such as this and knew they would have choices, some autonomy, and time to work together. Mrs. Cho used the three questions to purposely select meaningful content for this lesson, employ motivational elements, and use a constructivist teaching strategy to help her students discover the diversity of language.

- What is the important content I need to teach? (Diversity of language and its impact on vocabulary, spelling, and pronunciation)
- How am I going to motivate my students to learn it? (Teacher interest, appropriate challenge, cooperative learning)
- What teaching strategies will accomplish this? (Word sort, word hunt, group work)

Mrs. Cho modeled her interest in the topic and challenged students to think about some relevant questions and notice new words at home without promising a reward or threatening with a grade. Mrs. Cho knew that many students will extend their schoolwork "after hours" when they have been motivated but not coerced. She provided autonomy for the students to explore the words and allowed pairs and groups to think and talk together.

LEARNER EVENT—FLUENCY

The three components of fluency, as listed by the NRP (National Institute of Child Health and Human Development, 2000), are speed, accuracy, and appropriate expression. Fluency is related to reading comprehension in that readers who are fluent can direct more of their attention to understanding the text (Johns & Berglund, 2006). Johns and Berglund also note that fluency is often difficult for struggling readers. Their reading does not have the smooth, well-paced, vocal expression of proficient readers, so fluency instruction can be an important link to increased comprehension.

Just as phonemic awareness, phonics, and vocabulary building are tools that help students unlock the meaning of print, fluency as well should be presented to students in the context of print so the focus is on comprehension and not simply reading fast. Rereading is a well-recognized strategy to help cultivate fluency by improving word recognition, speed, and vocal expression. However, rereading needs to be used thoughtfully, paying attention to the meaningfulness and appropriateness of the chosen text.

The following lesson demonstrates fluency instruction with a real-life connection to increase motivation. Mr. Farlow had noticed that many of his seventh-grade students struggled with reading comprehension not only in their content-area textbooks but also with the novels they were reading in his language arts class.

He knew about the important connection between fluency and comprehension, but working on fluency with middle schoolers was difficult because they were easily embarrassed and shied away from reading aloud in class, or even just to him. He talked with his students candidly about the issues they were facing with comprehending what they read and about the connection research has found between comprehension and fluency.

Then Mr. Farlow visited the local nursing home facility and talked with the administrator about bringing some of his students to read aloud to the residents. This would give his students a real reason to read aloud and provide a service to the elderly residents as well. The administrator was very welcoming and went about finding which residents would benefit most from the read-alouds. She came up with eight residents who enjoyed stories but could not read themselves because of blindness or mild Alzheimer's disease.

Picture This in the Classroom . . .

Mr. Farlow went back to his classroom and called his twenty-two students together (he would try this project with just one of his classes at first—the lowest in comprehension and fluency).

"Good morning, everyone. I have some news for you. You know we have been talking about the importance of fluency, and I have a project that I think will be interesting for you and help you practice your fluency at the same time. It is also important because you will be participating in community service—putting something back into the community. I know you did some community service in your social studies class and felt good about what you did. This community service project is optional, however. If you are uncomfortable with it, you can choose another project option.

There are some people in our community who love stories and books but can't read. They are elderly and live at the Community Nursing Facility."

"Why can't they read?"

"They have Alzheimer's disease or are blind," replies Mr. Farlow. "But we can go over there during the school day and read to them. We'll practice here, and when we're ready, we'll go over and you can demonstrate your fluency and do a good deed too."

Several students registered some hesitancy and a discussion of Alzheimer's disease and blindness resulted. Mr. Farlow listened to the students' concerns, answered their questions, and encouraged a couple of students who wanted to research Alzheimer's disease.

"My grandma has Alzheimer's," says one student.

"My mom visits her uncle who has Alzheimer's. She says it's hard, but she'd want someone to visit her if she had it."

"I think this is a win-win situation," says Mr. Farlow. "We benefit by improving our fluency and comprehension. They benefit from your attention and the stories you read."

Mr. Farlow tells the students about the eight residents that the administrator had chosen for the project. There were seven women and one man. The man and one of the women are interested in the Civil War. Another woman loves animals. A couple of the women enjoy romance stories and one likes mysteries.

"I'm going to send you off to brainstorm about how you would like to accomplish this project," says Mr. Farlow. "You can work with a partner or a small group up to four members. Let me know if you want a different project option. Otherwise, we'll touch base with your ideas in fifteen minutes."

One student decides to read aloud to a kindergarten class instead of at the nursing home facility, but the rest of the class is anxious to discuss their ideas.

The twenty-one students divide themselves into five groups of three students and three groups of two students, trying to match their reading interests with those of the eight residents. They decide to find short stories, magazine articles, and/or poetry that can be read to the residents in one sitting.

Mr. Farlow gives them class time to locate reading materials, read them silently, and make choices. Then he gives them a strategy for practicing, which happens daily in class for a week.

"You have to have a strategy for practicing your read-alouds, a strategy that can help you rehearse your fluency," says Mr. Farlow. "All performers rehearse—musicians, dancers, soccer players. What are some things that you think you can do to rehearse fluency?"

"Rereading."

"Looking at punctuation marks."

"Knowing all the words."

"Making sure it makes sense."

"Putting expression in your voice."

"Yes, these are all very important, and we'll be working on all of them," says Mr. Farlow. "Let's start with simply reading through the pieces. You've already read them silently, which is crucial, but this time read them aloud. I think you have divided your pieces among your group members. Take time right now and read your pieces aloud to each other. It will be noisy in here, but that's okay. Find a corner where you can concentrate and begin."

After everyone is finished, Mr. Farlow asks for their attention.

"You have read your piece once and you've set a baseline. Now I want you to reread. While you are rereading, the others in your group will jot down all the places where you have increased your fluency. Go."

"What are the things that improved during your rereadings?" asks Mr. Farlow a little later.

"I knew all the words except one this time."

"Everything in the article makes sense to me now."

"I paid attention to question marks and commas more."

"I found some patterns in my story."

"There were some words that I emphasized the second time."

"I decided some words are more important than others."

"These are great observations," says Mr. Farlow. "Let's use them as we continue to rehearse over the next few days."

The next day, Mr. Farlow continues. "I want everyone to reread their piece again silently. As you do, underline or highlight any text feature that will help you read expressively, such as important words, question or exclamation marks, patterns that are repeated, and any other interesting words or phrases to emphasize. At the same time, check for problem areas. Circle any words you still struggle with or any part that doesn't make sense to you yet. Then we'll compare our experiences again."

After reading silently, the students discuss their findings.

"I still have a couple of words I'm not sure how to pronounce."

"Yeah, me too. This last paragraph is a little crazy. Can I change a word?"

"I found a lot of exclamation marks in mine."

"I'm not sure which words to emphasize."

"Mine is pretty emotional. I'm trying to put emotion in my voice."

"Okay," Mr. Farlow says. "You've brought up some good things that need to be rehearsed. I will meet with each group individually to help you sort out any pronunciation or meaning issues. I think it is appropriate to change a word or two to make a piece easier for you to read and easier for your listener to understand. I'll help you with that, too. But what about emotion? How do you put feeling in your reading? Let me give you some suggestions.

First, watch your pace. Choose some phrases or passages to read more slowly. Which ones would you choose?"

"Ones that are sad or ones that might be hard to understand."

"In a mystery, it might be the place where there is a clue."

"My story is about the Civil War. I think I might slow down on the names. There are names of so many generals."

"Good," says Mr. Farlow. "Good examples. Which passages might you read faster?"

"An exciting part!"

"Maybe dialogue, if you think the character would talk fast."

"You've got the idea!" says Mr. Farlow. "Another thing to consider is pausing. Where would you insert pauses? Maybe you can mark those with a slash. We're out of time for today, but we'll start with rereadings in our groups first thing tomorrow."

On the day before the trip to the nursing home facility, Mr. Farlow reminds students about marking pauses and working on pace and expression, and the students go to work in their groups. Mr. Farlow circulates and helps students with any concerns they have.

Finally, a "dress rehearsal" is held. Each group reads their piece to the rest of the class. Feedback sheets (like the one below) are filled out by the students for each group.

Changes of pace depending on the text	1	2	3
Expressive reading	1	2	3
Good use of pauses	1	2	3
Evident comprehension of the text	1	2	3

1 (ready to go to the nursing home)
2 (rehearse a little more)
3 (see Mr. Farlow for suggestions)

Last-minute preparations are made, and the students proclaim themselves ready for the trip.

The read-alouds at the nursing home are a success. The students are confident in their reading and are able to converse about the texts with their elderly partners. One group even decides to continue the project with a novel, returning to the nursing home to read to their partner on a regular basis.

Back in the classroom, Mr. Farlow has an important connection he wants the students to make.

"All right. You have successfully mastered fluently reading a text. How does this help you with comprehension? How can this help you read your science textbook, for example?"

"Now I pay attention to punctuation more and it helps me think about the meaning."

"If a text is hard, I try reading it out loud with expression."

"Some things I can read fast, others I have to slow down."

"If I can't read something fluently, I know I need to ask questions to help me understand it."

"I've been reading aloud to the little girl I babysit, and I think my fluency is getting better and better."

Mr. Farlow smiles. "You all have great ideas! Good job. We'll continue to work on fluency strategies in class throughout the year to help you with your comprehension."

Mr. Farlow was aware that practicing fluency can be tedious and boring for students. He thoughtfully planned a series of lessons based on the three questions:

- What is the important content to teach? (Fluency to improve comprehension)
- How am I going to motivate my students to learn it? (Meaningful, real-life practice and demonstration, informative feedback)
- What teaching strategies will accomplish this? (Brainstorming, group work, direct instruction to support students' learning, and service learning)

Mr. Farlow planned a project that gave his students authentic practice with fluency and the opportunity to help others and feel pride in their accomplishments. No need for extrinsic rewards here! The students received their intrinsic rewards from emotional involvement with their elderly partners. Each read-aloud truly made a difference in the lives of these nursing home residents; it was a selfless act on the part of the students, especially for those who struggled with reading.

The project provided appropriate challenge, allowed student choice of partners and text of interest, and required collaboration. Then, instead of simply telling students how to practice fluency, Mr. Farlow drew upon their prior knowledge and experiences, using them to help students understand fluency and its connection to increased comprehension. He knows this is how students learn.

The students constructed their own knowledge of the uses and benefits of fluency in their reading. Mr. Farlow also included meaningful feedback in the lesson. He and the students provided informative, yet supportive feedback about the read-alouds during the "dress rehearsal"—feedback meant not for evaluation but to sincerely help students use their fluency successfully at the nursing home.

LEARNER EVENT—COMPREHENSION

Capturing the meaning of "reading comprehension" can be difficult indeed. It is an abstract concept that is problematic to define and assess. Each individual reader may comprehend a specific text a different way based on interest, goal orientation, attitudes, perceived self-efficacy, motivations, and previous experience with text. Some definitions of comprehension describe meaning as existing only in the text and that it is the reader's job to unlock, or comprehend, the written message. Many of our students today, unfortunately, look at reading just this way.

However, the NRP (National Institute of Child Health and Human Development, 2000) uses a different definition, which states that explicit teaching should focus on helping students apply cognitive and metacognitive strategies that assist them in meaning-making, not just to unlock text, but to engage with it by making connections, synthesizing, asking questions, visualizing, inferring, developing predictions and opinions, and using the text in their own lives. These strategies are especially important when comprehension breaks down.

The beauty of the literature circles in the next lesson is that they are a real-life activity. Adults participate in similar book clubs, including Oprah! A major goal is to show students how literature circles can be a part of their lives on into adulthood. This last lesson highlights a third-grade classroom using literature circles to perceive deep meaning in text in a way that would also be appropriate for adult book clubs.

Picture This in the Classroom . . .

Ms. Marchand had chosen five nonfiction books for her students to read in literature circles. The five books all relate to "conflict," the theme being studied in class. Topics of the books include the Revolutionary War, unsolved crime mysteries, sibling rivalry, environmental sustainability, and endangered species. Two of the books are picture books with extensive text and three are short chapter books.

Ms. Marchand knew some of her third graders would feel more comfortable with pictures or photos to accompany the text, while others had embraced chapter books as a symbol of their progressing literacy. She collected multiple copies of each book and gave book talks on each title to her class.

The students had time to browse the books and ask questions. Ms. Marchand encouraged them to use the book previewing skills they had learned, such as reading the back of the book and first paragraph, noting the size of the print and the amount of white space on the pages, and reading a random page to count the number of words they didn't know. She then directed them to use an index card to write their top three choices, ranked in order.

Later, during her planning time, Ms. Marchand used the index cards to create groups. The students' interest in a particular book was her number-one consideration, but she also looked at student personalities and reading abilities to ensure group success.

The next day, Ms. Marchand passed out the books.

"I looked at the choices you put on your index cards and now I'm going to give you your book. I know everyone didn't get their first choice, but I worked hard to give you the book you rated number one or number two. If you didn't get your number-one choice, you can always read that book later in the year. All the books will go into our classroom library."

The students spent a couple of minutes previewing their books and then Ms. Marchand passed out a pad of sticky notes for each student.

"You're going to start reading today. Remember how we've done literature circles before? With role sheets? Well, you're not going to use role sheets, but you're going to use the strategies you learned through role sheets. You will use the sticky notes I just handed out. Knowing that, what do you think you could write on these sticky notes?"

"Well, we wrote questions about the book on the role sheets."

"Yes," says Ms. Marchand. "You could write a question you have as you're reading, and with sticky notes you can put the note right on the text where you have the question."

"We could do that with connections, too."

"And with interesting vocabulary words . . . and words we don't know."

"And things that surprise us."

"Predictions."

"Something we don't want to forget."

"Clues if it's a mystery."

"It's too bad we can't draw."

"Oh, but you can draw!" says Ms. Marchand. "If one sticky note is too small, put several notes together on a page to hold your drawing."

"Can we just put a question mark if we have a question or an exclamation point if something surprises us?"

"No," says Ms. Marchand. "Remember, the point of your notes is two-fold. First, you want to record your thinking and that will take more than a question mark. Second, you need to remember your thoughts so you can share them with your group. This looks like a good time to go over how we will organize our literature circles."

Ms. Marchand has the students meet in their groups to divide their books in half. They will read half the book, and then meet for literature circles in two days. They will have another two days to finish their books, and then there will be a second literature circle.

As they read, the students use their sticky notes to draw and write questions, predictions, summaries, inferences, and connections. They place them directly on the text they are reading. Ms. Marchand talks with them about doing the most they can do to ensure successful literature circles, not the least they can do, and she gives them time to read independently in class. She chooses one of the books herself to read, using sticky notes to comment as well.

When it is time for the first literature circle, Ms. Marchand has the groups get together with their books. Her one requirement is that they all have their books open, looking at the text as they discuss their books. When the students had first come into the classroom that morning, she had personally asked one student from each group to begin the discussion with a question they had about the book.

"Is everyone ready? It looks to me like all the groups are together. Great. Dig into your book!"

Ms. Marchand walks around the room making sure all the groups get started smoothly. Eventually, she joins the group that is reading the same book as she is. She participates carefully, making sure to avoid facilitating the group.

Ms. Marchand is aware when the discussion starts to dwindle and gaps of quiet or chatting take its place.

"All right, everyone. Take two more minutes to discuss this last question. What would you rate your book on a scale of one to five, with five being the best. And why did you choose that rating? Make sure to record your rating so you can compare it with the rating you give the book when you've completed it."

When the discussion dies down, Ms. Marchand leads the class through a self-evaluation of their circles. What was the most successful thing about your circle's discussion? What will you change for the next circle? Students record their answers as goals to use the next time.

"Enjoy finishing your books!" Ms. Marchand tells her students, and gives them time to read and write sticky notes when they return to their seats.

The second literature circle is run in the same manner. Students are reminded to look at their goals, which they set at the end of the first circles. To conclude this session of literature circles, Ms. Marchand asks each group to present a three-sentence summary of their book (without giving too much away!) along with a rating so other students could choose some of these books to read during Sustained Silent Reading. She then collects the students' books and uses the sticky notes for assessment.

Using literature circles is a strategy to help students organize and record their thoughts about their reading. This is important because it enables them to participate well in a group discussion where the goal is to enhance their comprehension of the text, just as in adult book clubs. Ms. Marchand used the three questions to structure her lesson:

- What is the important content I need to teach? (Comprehension of text, discussion skills)
- How am I going to motivate my students to learn it? (Choice of literature, cooperative learning, informative feedback from peers, teacher interest, appropriate challenge)
- What teaching strategies will accomplish this? (Small-group literature circles)

Ms. Marchand knows that students are motivated by working with their peers cooperatively and receiving feedback from them. She promotes informative, and not judgmental, feedback by helping students set goals and then experience success in meeting these goals. She shows her own interest in the process by choosing a book and participating in the circles herself, yet she is careful to allow an appropriate amount of autonomy to the groups.

Literature circles inherently provide choice and meaningful work as well as foster the inclusion of all voices better than in a whole class setting. When students feel they "belong," that their opinions are listened and responded to, and that they are supported to really dig into a text, intrinsic motivation to engage in the task and involve themselves emotionally removes much of the need to reward for good work or to punish for bad behavior.

CONCLUSION

Teachers of reading have two goals: (1) to accomplish the district, state, and federal initiatives put before them, and (2) to motivate their students to be strategic, lifelong readers.

Infuse your lessons with motivation. Sneak motivational elements into everything you teach. Make it your default drive. Teaching for the test or for the grade or for the pizza is just a means to an end, and that end is often minimized or overlooked. The end itself is meaningful—enjoyable reading— and *that* should be the core of all reading lessons. We must take our students past the grades and the worksheets and the tests and on into their lives as purposeful, successful, reflective, intrinsically motivated readers.

REFERENCES

Berger, R. (2003). *An ethic of excellence: Building a culture of craftsmanship with students.* Portsmouth, NH: Heinemann.

Calkins, L. M. (2001). *The art of teaching reading.* New York: Longman.

Fox, M. (2002). *The magic hat.* San Diego: Harcourt.

Glasser, W. (1998). *Choice theory: A new psychology of personal freedom.* New York: Harper-Collins.

Harris, T. L., & Hodges, R. E. (1995). *The literacy dictionary.* Newark, DE: International Reading Association.

Johns, J. L., & Berglund, R. L. (2006). *Fluency: Strategies and assessment* (3rd ed.). Dubuque, IA: Kendall/Hunt.

Kohn, A. (1996). *Beyond discipline.* Alexandria, VA: Association for Supervision and Curriculum Development.

Lenski, S. D., & Nierstheimer, S. L. (2004). *Becoming a teacher of reading.* Upper Saddle River, NJ: Pearson.

Malouf, D. (1983). Do rewards reduce student motivation? *School Psychology Review, 12*(1), 1–11.

Martin, B., Jr., & Archambault, J. (1989). *Chicka chicka boom boom.* New York: Simon & Schuster.

McGee, L. M., & Richgels, D. J. (2008). *Literacy's beginnings: Supporting young readers and writers* (5th ed.). Boston: Pearson.

Morrow, L. M. (2002). *The literacy center.* Portland, ME: Stenhouse.

National Institute of Child Health and Human Development (2000). *Report of the National Reading Panel. Teaching children to read: An evidence-based assessment of the scientific research literature on reading and its implications for reading instruction* (NIH Publication No. 00-4769). Washington, DC: U.S. Government Printing Office.

Oldfather, P., & Dahl, K. (1994). Toward a social constructivist reconceptualization of intrinsic motivation for literacy learning. *Journal of Reading Behavior, 26,* 139–58.

Pressley, M., Dolezal, S., Raphael, L., Mohan, L., Roehrig, A., & Bogner, K. (2003). *Motivating primary-grade students.* New York: The Guilford Press.

Smith, F. (1997). *Reading without nonsense* (3rd ed.). New York: Teachers College Press.

Waber, B. (1972). *Ira sleeps over.* Boston: Houghton Mifflin.

Wadsworth, B. J. (2004). *Piaget's theory of cognitive and affective development.* Boston: Pearson.

Teaching Memoir: The First Day

Anonymous

I know the exact day I became a constructivist teacher.

The principal who had just hired me was walking me down the hall to the classroom that would be mine in just a few days. I was feeling joyful, anxious, and incredulous all at the same time: I would soon be a seventh- and eighth-grade language arts teacher. My career was off to a grand start.

As we walked into the room, I noticed its spaciousness, wide windows, and that precious smell that seems to linger in all schools; the scent of students past and present filling the desks and eager to learn. I felt at home.

"I'm sorry," said the principal.

"It's a great room," I protested.

"No, I mean about the books."

"What books?"

"That's exactly it. We could only afford to purchase the reading series for grades K–6. I'm sorry you have no textbooks."

"Oh. That's all right. I'll work it out," I said, so new to teaching that I thought anything was possible.

And that year went well. I cobbled together some anthologies of short stories, purchased paperbacks from garage sales and Goodwill, and read aloud poetry, newspaper articles, book excerpts, and student writing.

We visited the library often where students could choose their own books to read in class.

I watched my students carefully and talked with them often about the authors they loved and those they didn't. I brought in literature I thought would intrigue them and paid attention to their opinions. We wrote about our reading and we read to inform our writing. Tests were taken when appropriate and the answers were discussed and debated. I knew my students' strengths and struggles and I planned our days accordingly.

We never missed the textbooks.

Several years later, I moved to a first-grade classroom in the same district. As a special favor to the teachers, the secretary had agreed to run off all the worksheets needed each week and deliver them to each teacher's classroom on Fridays. I was stunned the first time she came to my door with a stack of papers a foot high.

The only thing I could think of to do was to come to school on Saturday and stealthily deposit the worksheets in the dumpster behind the building. I hated to be accused of wasting paper, but I had no intention of using these worksheets to teach.

It was then that I realized what teaching is all about. The publisher of these worksheets had never met my students. I, on the other hand, knew them inside and out. I knew Kelly liked Eric Carle's illustrations and Michael preferred nonfiction and Jayla loved any book her best friend loved. I knew who struggled with phonics and whose parents read to them every night. I knew that the class liked working on math puzzles, but they didn't like games that had one winner. I knew they learned if I made connections to their lives and showed them why school was important. Designing curriculum was *my* job, not the publisher's job.

The philosophy of social constructivism was introduced to me much later in my career. What a discovery it was that there was actually research to support what I already believed! Even today, I travel on the continuum that is constructivist teaching. Sometimes the way is easy and enjoyable, and other times the road is steep with potholes. Being a teacher and a learner that holds a constructivist philosophy is inspiring and challenging, and I wouldn't have it any other way.

Chapter Seven

Developing Curriculum for the Constructivist Classroom

Patti L. Sandy

When you enter a constructivist classroom, whether it be at the primary, middle, or high school level, you won't find piles of textbooks with students answering questions at the end of a chapter. You won't see desks lined up neatly in rows or hear the teacher lecturing from the front of the room. Don't bother to look for workbooks. Materials won't be stacked in plastic bins on shelves collecting dust. Instead, you'll find a teacher who facilitates learning events for students to construct their own knowledge. You'll find students working individually or in small groups to find answers to questions that they've posed based on their interests, past experiences, and prior knowledge.

One of the biggest differences between traditional and constructivist classrooms is the curriculum. Most traditional classrooms use purchased curriculum materials that include teacher manuals containing scripted lesson plans and a textbook or workbook for each subject area. Every grade in the district uses the same materials and they are often on the same teaching schedule. Sometimes, you'll find students in different parts of the United States doing the same lesson on the same day. *"It's day 23 so we must be on lesson 23, regardless of whether the students are ready for it or not."*

No two constructivist classrooms are alike, because the students in each classroom are unique, have different backgrounds and interests, and want to learn different things. Students don't come from cookie-cutters, and neither can curriculum. Knowing that ready-made curricula won't meet all the needs in the classroom, how does a busy teacher go about writing curriculum for his or her students? A unit is a working document; it should be continuously revised to meet the interests, prior knowledge, needs, and important questions that students want answered.

This chapter focuses on a sample science unit on *Living Things and Their Environments* for first-grade students, although this unit model will work with any content area. You can organize your curriculum by using a thick three-ring binder with dividers. Your curriculum binder will have the following twelve sections.

STATE STANDARDS

The first step in writing curriculum is to look carefully at your state and the national standards to find out what students need to learn for your grade level. This is the foundation of a curriculum. Often, the standards span multiple grade levels. Collaborate with colleagues to determine what standards or parts of standards would be covered at each grade level, *making sure that all standards are met.*

Several standards can be combined into one unit. Copy these standards and put them into the first section of the curriculum binder. Study the standards carefully, pulling out the declarative knowledge (what students need to learn) and procedural knowledge (how students will learn it). Declarative knowledge is identified by the nouns in the standards. The procedural knowledge is identified by the verbs in the standards, such as conduct, explore, examine, participate, select, identify, investigate, construct, discuss, observe, collect, record, and chart.

CONTENT SUMMARY

After marking the declarative knowledge in the standards, thoroughly research these topics, using multiple sources. This will take time and effort, but it is an important step in the process of writing curriculum. The teacher needs extensive knowledge of the content to be taught. Be sure to keep track of what resources you use and record them at the end of your binder.

Next, write a content summary to put in the next section of the curriculum binder. This is a written narrative of the essential information found in the standards for the unit, and not just an outline. The length will vary based on the standards. Everything in the standard(s) for the unit should be covered in the content summary. The content summary is not something just cut and pasted from a website or sentences copied from a book. Take what you learn from your research and put it into your own words. *This will give you ownership of your curriculum.*

DEFINITIONS

For the next section of the curriculum binder go back to your content summary, highlight all of the nouns, and carefully define each word in a sentence. Use your resource materials to help you construct definitions that give complete information, but in simple, easy to understand language.

Define each word as if you did not know what it meant previously. It is also crucial that you define key words in your definitions. *Someone with no prior knowledge of your unit should be able to pick up your content summary and list of definitions of key words and understand fully what students will learn from your unit.* Send a copy of the definitions home along with the content summary. Don't assume that parents know everything you're teaching.

CONCEPT MAPS

The curriculum binder should contain at least one, but sometimes several, concept maps. These are graphic organizers that can be created either by hand or in a computer program such as *Inspiration*. The "Big Concept," also referred to as "Big Idea," for your unit goes at the top of your concept map (Living Things/Nonliving Things). On the level below that, break it down to the next smaller concepts (Vertebrates/Invertebrates). Continue making layers on your concept map, using arrows to show interrelationships between the concepts. It is important to remember that concepts are not taught in isolation, but rather as part of a whole.

Some teachers begin making concept maps at a whiteboard with an eraser handy, while other teachers work on their computers. Ask colleagues for feedback on the different versions of your concepts maps. They will likely see interrelationships that you might miss. It's a good idea to send home a copy of your concept map(s) to parents; it gives them a quick snapshot of what concepts you'll be teaching in your unit.

Concept mapping helps you, as the teacher, truly learn the material before teaching it to students. *You will be confident in your content knowledge and will enjoy imparting your knowledge to students.*

FOCUS QUESTIONS

Inquiry is the backbone of a constructivist classroom. We want students to develop questions around the Big Idea, and construct answers to these questions during the learning events. This will lead to new questions being posed, and *the learning cycle will continue on and on as we help students on their journey to becoming lifelong learners.*

When a unit is introduced, we find out what students already know about the topic. This makes a great chart for your classroom. Next, find out what students want to learn about the topic. What are they curious about? What do they wonder about? Record the questions your students have and display them in your classroom. When you find out the answers, write them down on the chart, too.

Teachers need to develop their own focus questions for the unit as well. These are the ones that usually are recorded in this section of the curriculum binder. Make sure that you have several focus questions for each cell on your concept map. Focus questions should be sent home for parents. Some example focus questions from the unit are:

- What do living things need to survive in a habitat?
- What does it mean when we say an animal is a vertebrate or invertebrate?
- What characteristics do all mammals (reptiles, amphibians, birds, fish) have in common and how are they different from other animals?
- What adaptations does an animal have to help it survive in its habitat?
- What happens to animals that don't adapt to an environment?
- Why do some reptiles shed their skin?

LEARNER OUTCOMES

Learner outcomes are statements that specify what learners should know or be able to do at the conclusion of a unit. When writing learner outcomes, ask yourself these key questions: "What is the essential information I want my students to know?" and "What specific skills or strategies do my students need to be able to do?" There are several important characteristics of good learner outcomes:

- The outcome must state who is participating.
- The outcome must state what action they are taking.
- The outcome must state what will result from their action.
- The action by the learner must be observable.
- The action by the learner must be measurable.

Don't use verbs in the outcomes that aren't measurable, such as "know," "appreciate," "learn," "understand." Better verbs to use in outcomes are "design," "develop," "revise," "plan," "prepare," "explain," "discuss," "critique," "analyze," and so on. Another common mistake is to confuse learner outcomes with grade-level goals or objectives, which is what students should *know*. Learner outcomes address what students will *do*. Students and their parents need to know what the learner outcomes are at the beginning of each unit. Send a copy home and keep them posted on your class website. Some sample learner outcomes from this unit follow. *Notice that the essential information appears first and the skill or strategy used to assess this outcome comes second. This ensures that the outcomes focus on important knowledge and not peripheral skills.*

- The students will sort sets of animal pictures by their characteristics and explain their decisions to a partner.
- The students will demonstrate knowledge of the complete life cycle of a frog by creating a poster.
- The students will compare and contrast reptiles and amphibians by completing a Venn diagram.

SCHEDULE OF INVESTIGATIONS

Constructivist classrooms don't have schedules written in stone. A teacher must be flexible to follow the interests and needs of the students. Make a tentative schedule based on the number of weeks you think the unit might take. Creating a large overview of a unit first (or even a year's worth of units) and then breaking the unit into daily activities can facilitate planning. *This may be especially important if you are teaching in a traditional school and are fitting in constructivist units around other required lessons.*

STUDENT INVESTIGATIONS AND LESSONS

This section of your unit binder contains lesson plans using instructional models for a constructivist classroom, such as (1) Concept Formation, (2) Concept Attainment, (3) Student-Generated Inquiry, and (4) Social Interaction

Concept Formation is the process of extending and refining concepts present from the learner's prior understanding. It seeks to categorize and generalize. Instruction builds on what students already know, adding new information and supporting modification of this information. In this model, students form groups of concepts of related items and then try to explain with a generalization about how two or more of the groups relate to each other. A concept formation lesson asks students to list, group, label, regroup, and synthesize.

A Concept Attainment lesson involves looking at examples and nonexamples of the concept under study. Rather than the teacher simply defining a concept for students, the students work to define the concept themselves through examining and discussing patterns, exemplars, and contradictions.

Typically, when teachers decide to provide inquiry activities for students, they set up the parameters, determine the correct answers, and then allow the students to "discover" the solution. In Student-Generated Inquiry, however, the students follow a line of inquiry that interests them (most likely related to a unit being studied in class) and that may lead them to information not predetermined by the teacher. The students act as researchers and both students and teachers learn new things!

Social Interaction refers to student work done in pairs and small groups. While a classroom using lessons involving social interaction may be noisy and "look messy," in reality these lessons are highly structured and require students to produce work using higher-order thinking skills. The social interactions have content objectives, learner outcomes, and assessment of student work.

For samples of these four instructional models, see this chapter's appendixes.

ASSESSMENTS

A curriculum binder should include copies of all of the assessments and rubrics you use in your unit to monitor student learning. Include both formative and summative assessments.

Formative assessments inform teachers and students about the process of learning while that learning is taking place and are used as a tool for planning. Formative assessments, such as teacher checklists, anecdotal records, and student self-evaluations, diagnose student needs and help the teacher plan the next steps in instruction based on those needs.

Make plans to teach students how to self-assess and provide opportunities for students to reflect on their own learning and set goals. By including tools for student self-evaluation throughout the unit, you'll provide students with feedback they can use to improve the quality of their work during actual production. Teachers need to make plans in their curriculum to let students keep track of their work through portfolios and to communicate with others about their learning and progress.

Your unit should also include summative assessments to check that learning has occurred. They need to measure mastery of learner outcomes and content knowledge. We want to know if a student has the ability to use knowledge to reason and can demonstrate performance skills and product development capabilities. Traditionally, teachers have used selected-response, true/false, matching, short-answer, and fill-in questions on assessments. These types of assessments are rarely used in a constructivist classroom.

A more effective method of summative assessment would be to have a student construct an extended written response to a question rather than select one from a list. Points can be given for specific pieces of information that are present or a rubric can be used for scoring purposes. Performance assessments that engage students in an activity or task require them to apply a performance skill or create a product while the teacher observes and assesses quality are very appropriate to use.

Assessment is *for and of* learning. It can also be done through one-on-one conversations, class discussions, peer conferences, interviews, and student journals. Immediate feedback can be given from the teacher or classmates, and misconceptions can be cleared up as they occur. Keeping track of students' oral answers to questions prepared in advance can be accomplished through checklists, although some teachers find it better to videotape a discussion and review it later.

GUEST SPEAKERS/FIELD EXPERIENCES

Providing multiple opportunities for students to participate in hands-on activities and gain firsthand experiences will deepen their conceptual learning. It is important to find out what is available in your community and take advantage of all the resources available to you and your students. Even with budget cuts and limited field trips, it is possible to schedule guest speakers who are willing to come to your classroom free of charge.

This section of the curriculum binder is the place for you to keep track of all of your contacts for field trips and guest speakers. Be sure to list as much information as possible and include brochures, pamphlets, contact names, phone numbers, e-mail addresses, and so on.

Before you begin your unit, send parents a questionnaire to find out if they have any knowledge, collections, interests, or talents to share with your class as a guest speaker. This involves parents in their child's education. Parents might bring in animals, including different kinds of mammals, aquariums full of different kinds of fish, tarantulas, parakeets, and lots of snakes and lizards. Find "experts" on your unit topics in the community and ask them to share their expertise with your students.

My school is located less than fifteen minutes from a pond that has a nature center. While there, we hike through a meadow and forest with nets and magnifying glasses to find and classify invertebrates, such as insects and spiders, and vertebrates, such as mammals and birds. We use dip nets in the stream. Every student has the chance to put on waders and go seining in the pond. We learn so much about life cycles when we see and compare tadpoles and frogs. We use field manuals and the nature center guide to help us classify the amphibians, reptiles, and fish that we discover.

We are thirty minutes from the Delaware Bay and forty-five minutes from the Atlantic Ocean. My students have been able to have scavenger hunts along the bay and the ocean, investigating vertebrates, such as fish and birds, and invertebrates, such as horseshoe crabs, blue crabs, jellyfish, sea stars, univalves (snails, whelks, etc.), and bivalves (oysters, clams, mussels, etc.). We've witnessed dolphins jumping out of the water. Living so close to water allows us to become "experts" on animals living in or near fresh and saltwater habitats.

A benefit of field experiences is that they make students more curious about the world around them, and they motivate them to learn more about things on their own and with their friends and families. Students do additional research at home on an animal that interests them, and they come back to school eager to share what they've learned. You just can't compare seeing an animal in person to reading about one or seeing a picture in a book.

INTEGRATED ACTIVITIES

How can you integrate the concepts you're teaching in your unit with other subject areas, music, art, physical education, and technology? Use the expertise of the specialists in your school to help design learning activities that integrate different content areas in a natural, authentic way rather than in isolation. Before beginning your unit, meet with everyone and share your content summary, concept map(s), and learner outcomes so that there is a clear picture of what you want students to learn from your unit.

Ask your colleagues to share their knowledge and help you design learning events that integrate across the curriculum. Some teachers include the integrated lesson plans in this section of the binder. Others keep track using some type of graphic organizer.

In the unit on Living Things in their Environments, the music teacher located songs about animals, and the art teacher helped students design props and scenery for skits and readers' theater. The art teacher also went with the class to the zoo and helped the students sketch many of the animals they saw. At school, students wrote sentences about each animal and created a class big book. Our Spanish teacher taught students the names of animals in Spanish, and in math, the students counted their favorite animals and created bar graphs.

The technology teacher helped the students learn how to find and access information about different animals from websites. She showed them how to import pictures and find clip art. She taught keyboarding and word processing to the students, and worked with them to research a specific animal that interested them. Some students made posters, while others made books. *The unit encompassed all content areas: science, language arts, math, geography, Spanish, the fine arts, physical education, and technology.*

TEACHER/STUDENT REFERENCE MATERIALS AND RESOURCES

In a constructivist classroom, teachers and students need access to a lot of different resources. This is the section to list everything that you and your students use for the unit, such as a bibliography of resource books and children's literature. Include the ISBN in case the book needs to be ordered in the future. List things that you used to write your content summary, definitions, develop your lessons and activities, and create your assessments. Don't forget to list DVDs, websites, and learning games.

SUMMARY

When teachers invest time and energy into writing their own curriculum rather than using a purchased one, they gain ownership of the curriculum. It is tailored to build on the prior knowledge of their students and meet their individual needs. The curriculum is fluid and changes according to need. Teachers who write their own curriculum find that their students are more actively engaged in learning and have a deeper understanding of the content knowledge.

Rather than memorizing random facts, students construct a deep understanding of the content knowledge. Learning is for the long term rather than the short term. Is writing your own curriculum more difficult than simply using a textbook curriculum? Yes, but the result is an increase in student learning, motivation, *and* test scores. You may even find that you, as the teacher, are enjoying your job ever so much more!

APPENDIX A: CONCEPT FORMATION LESSON PLAN: DIVERSITY OF ANIMALS

Content Summary

Many different kinds of animals live throughout the world. Animals can be sorted into groups in many ways using various properties to decide which things belong to which group; features for grouping depend on the purpose for the grouping. For example, animals can be classified or sorted into groups based on appearance and behaviors.

Animals come in many shapes and sizes. Some have blowholes for breathing, claws, or beaks. Different types of animals live in different places in the world. Animals have external features that help them survive in different environments. Animals have a variety of external protection, such as fur, hair, dry or moist skin, or feathers. Some animals eat plants, some eat other animals, and some eat both. Some animals have sharp teeth, while others have flat teeth, and yet other animals do not have any teeth at all. Some animals burrow and other build nests. There are animals that lay eggs and those that give birth.

Animals can sleep at night, during the day, or both. Animals can hibernate, migrate, or use camouflage to protect themselves against predators. Some animals go through changes in their appearance as the seasons change. Animals depend on one another and on the environment for survival.

Learner Outcomes

By the end of the lesson the student will be able to:

- Participate as a class to name different animals to be written on the board by the teacher.
- Participate as a class to group and regroup the animals on the board based on similarities and differences in their appearance and behavior, create labels for the groups, and explain the relationships between the animals.

Learner Activities

Advance Organizer

The students are asked to come to the carpet area and be seated. The teacher helps students connect learning to prior knowledge.

- Listing: The teacher says to the class, *"I want you to tell me all of the different kinds of animals that you know. I'll write the names of the animals on the board when you tell them to me."* The teacher calls on students one at a time to name an animal and lists the names of the animals on the whiteboard.
- Grouping: The teacher says, *"Do any of these animals belong together? Read the names of all of the animals that we wrote on the whiteboard and think about it for a few minutes. Raise your hands and tell me animals that have things in common. I'll group them together by circling their names with colored markers."* The teacher uses a different colored marker for each group.
- Labeling: The teacher points to the newly formed groups and says, *"What would you call these groups that you just made?"* The students are given time to generate labels for each group. The teacher writes the labels for each group on the whiteboard. The teacher then asks, *"Why would you group the different animals together like this? Explain to us why you put certain animals together in the same group."* The students take turns identifying and verbalizing the common characteristics of the animals in each group.
- Regrouping: Next, the teacher encourages students to state different relationships between individual animals or whole groups of animals by asking, *"Could some of these animals belong in more than one group? Look to see if there are animals in one group that you could put in another group."* After this the teacher asks, *"Are there whole groups that you could be placed under one of the other labels? Why would you group them that way?"*
- Synthesizing: *"Can someone say in one sentence something about all of these groups?"* The students are asked to pair up with a partner or a small group to summarize the data and form generalizations by making a general statement about animal diversity. The teacher may need to first demonstrate how to do this by giving an example of a summary statement.

Closure

Conclusions are discussed regarding the concept of the diversity of animals and their relationship with one another. Students are given the opportunity to research an animal using a book or the Internet and report back to the class on their learning.

Assessment of Learning

Use of the following rubric can guide the teacher's assessment of student learning and provide specific feedback for students.

Table 7.1. Rubric for Diversity of Animals Concept Formation Lesson

	0	1	2	3	4
Persistence	Never attempts	Attempts but gives up quickly	Attempts but stops at first issue	Attempts and works through some issues	Does not give up until all issues are resolved
Reflection	Never uses past knowledge or experience to form new understanding	Rarely uses past knowledge or experience to form new understanding	Frequently uses past knowledge or experience to form new understanding	Occasionally uses past knowledge or experience to form new understanding	Always uses past knowledge or experience to form new understanding
Self-Direction	Refuses direction	Needs constant individual attention	Needs frequent reminders and direction or redirection	Works with minimal direction with only occasional reminders	Works independently and initiates further responsibility
Listing	Does not list any animals	Lists only one or two animals	Lists a few animals	Lists several animals	Lists many animals
Grouping/Regrouping/Labeling	Does not group any animals or provide any labels	Makes only a few obvious groups with labels	Generates a few creative groups with labels	Generates several creative groups with labels and explanations	Generates many creative groups with labels and explanations
Generalizations Made From Relationships in Grouping Process	Does not make generalizations	Makes at least one simple generalization	Makes more than one simple generalizations	Makes at least one complex generalization	Makes two or more complex generalizations

APPENDIX B: CONCEPT ATTAINMENT LESSON PLAN: MAMMALS

Content Summary

Animals include mammals, reptiles, amphibians, birds, and fish. Mammals are everywhere—in the sea, on land, and in the air. But what makes a mammal a mammal is a number of defining characteristics that its neighbors in the water, air, and on land don't have. There are about 5,400 species of mammals. People are mammals.

The word "mammal" is derived from "mammary glands." All mammals have mammary glands to nurse their young. They are vertebrates, which means that they have backbones. They are warm blooded and have highly developed brains. They breathe with lungs and have hair on their bodies. Though many other animals share many of these traits, mammals are the only animals with mammary glands and hair. Different mammals have specialized characteristics. For example, the porcupine has sharp, spiny hairs called quills that it uses to ward off predators.

There are three different ways that mammals are born. Most baby mammals, like humans, grow inside the mother until they are ready to be born. But marsupials, like kangaroos and koalas, are born very tiny and must crawl into their mother's pouch in order to continue their development. There are a few kinds of mammals that lay eggs. But no matter how their young are born, mammal mothers typically take care of them for a long time and teach them how to survive. Mammals have fewer young than other species in large part because of the time and energy it takes to care for them.

Mammals have more advanced brains than other animals, making them the most intelligent animals on Earth. Some mammals, like humans and monkeys, have developed opposable thumbs and can use them to make tools, while others have unique ways of finding food.

Most mammals live on land. However, some mammals live in the sea. These marine mammals include whales, dolphins, porpoises, and sea lions. These mammals differ from other animals that live in water because they breathe with lungs. They must come to the surface to get air. Most aquatic animals, such as fish, extract oxygen from the water using gills and must stay under water at all times in order to live. The only mammal that can spend time in the air and fly is the bat. Most other animals that can fly are birds.

Learner Outcomes

By the end of the lesson the student will be able to:

- From a group of animals, identify which are mammals, and which are not, based on their characteristics.
- Name and explain the unique characteristics of mammals.
- Identify mammals that live on the land, in water, and can fly in the air.

Learner Activities

Advance Organizer

The students are seated on the carpet. The teacher leads a group discussion to tap prior knowledge and review what students have learned previously about the characteristics of birds, fish, reptiles, and amphibians. The lesson will introduce mammals to the students.

- Students are directed to their tables. Each student is given a plastic reclosable bag containing about fifteen pictures of different animals, including mammals, birds, fish, reptiles, and amphibians. They are asked to find a way to sort them.
- Students explain and discuss their categories, first in small groups at their table with four or five students and then with the whole class.
- The teacher introduces the term "mammal" by explaining that it comes from the words "mammary glands." Students are asked to think of animals that feed their babies with their milk. Students are asked to re-sort their pictures with this characteristic. Students share as a class what animals they have that are mammals. Teacher observation of student responses allows for formative assessment. The teacher provides feedback and addresses any misconceptions to ensure that the student responses are correct, and reinforces why each animal is or is not a mammal.
- Students look at their categories and share as a class what other characteristics mammals have (backbones, warm blooded, hair, breathe with lungs, well-developed brain, usually born live). The teacher lists these characteristics on a chart as they are identified by the class.
- Students are asked to re-sort only the pictures of mammals by where they live. Students discuss their sorting as a class.
- The categories of "land," "water," and "can fly in the air" are given by the teacher, and students re-sort the pictures. Students discuss their sorting as a class. Next, students name other mammals that live on land and in water, noting that the bat is the only mammal that can fly.
- The teacher holds up several new pictures of animals for the class to sort based on their new knowledge of the characteristics of mammals, including unusual animals that live in the water, such as a sea lion, porpoise, and dolphin, and different kinds of bats that live in the air and fly.

Closure

Students may choose to do at least one of the following follow-up activities:

- Look through magazines and cut out pictures of mammals to create a poster. Use pictures cut from magazines or from your own illustrations. Then, create a poster with sections showing mammals that live on land, in the water, and in the air.
- Write a story and draw an illustration of your favorite mammal.
- Write separate lists of all the names of mammals you can think of that live on land, in water, and can fly.
- Choose a mammal to research. Find a way to share what you learned with your classmates.

Assessment

Students are given a sheet with pictures and the names of twelve different animals that include mammals, bird, fish, reptiles, and amphibians. Students identify which are mammals by cutting out the pictures, sorting them, and gluing them on a separate sheet with the heading Mammals/Not Mammals. Next, students are asked to circle mammals that live on land with a green crayon, mammals that live in water with a blue crayon, and mammals that live in the air and fly with a red crayon. Finally, students individually talk with the teacher to explain their responses—that is, why each animal is or is not a mammal based on its characteristics, and where they live.

Table 7.2. Rubric for Concept Attainment Lesson on Mammals

	0	1	2	3	4
Persistence	Never attempts	Attempts but gives up quickly	Attempts but stops at first issue	Attempts and works through some issues	Does not give up until all issues are resolved
Reflection	Never uses past knowledge or experience to form new understanding	Rarely uses past knowledge or experience to form new understanding	Occasionally uses past knowledge or experience to form new understanding	Frequently uses past knowledge or experience to form new understanding	Always uses past knowledge or experience to form new understanding
Self-Direction	Refuses direction	Needs constant individual attention	Needs frequent reminders and direction or redirection	Works with minimal direction with only occasional reminders	Works independently and initiates further responsibility
Identification of Mammals	Cannot correctly identify any mammals	Correctly identifies one to three mammals	Correctly identifies four or five mammals	Correctly identifies six or seven mammals	Correctly identifies all twelve mammals
Identification of where each mammal lives	Cannot correctly identify where any mammals live	Correctly identifies where one to three mammals live	Correctly identifies where four to eight mammals live	Correctly identifies where nine to eleven mammals live	Correctly identifies where all twelve mammals live
Explanation of Categories (Mammals/Not Mammals)	Student cannot explain reasons for categories	Student can only explain very minimal reasons for categories	Student can explain a few reasons for categories	Student can accurately explain most of the reasons for categories	Student discusses reasons for categories, describing the sorting process

APPENDIX C: STUDENT-GENERATED INQUIRY MODEL: REPTILES (TURTLES AND TORTOISES, LIZARDS AND SNAKES)

Content Summary

There are five characteristics that make an animal a reptile:

- Reptiles are vertebrates (animals with a backbone)
- Reptiles are cold-blooded animals, which means they get their body heat from outside sources, for example, by basking in the sun or moving into warm areas. The temperature of the reptile's environment always dictates the temperature of the animal itself—when it is cold outside, the reptile's body is just as cold inside. When reptiles are active, they can be as warm as any bird or mammal. To cool down during the hottest part of the day, reptiles expose as little of their body as possible to the sun's rays, or they move into the shade. Reptiles come in many shapes and sizes and live in most habitats, from the oceans to the deserts. Most reptiles are found in tropical and subtropical areas, and not in the colder polar regions.
- Reptiles are covered with scales, which are dry and firm.
- Reptiles breathe air through the use of lungs.
- Reptiles lay eggs on land with a leathery protective shell, designed to protect the baby reptiles until they are ready to hatch.

Turtles and Tortoises

Turtles and tortoises are the only reptiles that have a shell built into the skeleton. Most turtles live in water, but tortoises live on land. Sea turtles live in the oceans and eat fish, jellyfish, sponges, crabs, clams, and marine plants such as seaweed. Sea turtles have large front flippers to push them quickly through the water. Males never leave the water and females do so only to lay eggs.

Freshwater turtles live in ponds, lakes, streams, and rivers. Pond turtles need to move on land and in the water, so they have webbing between their claws. The forty species of land tortoises have column-shaped legs with large claws to grip the earth. They are active only during the coolest times of the day. Turtles and tortoises have strong and heavy high-domed shells to protect them from predators. Their backbone is located on the inside of the shell. They move slowly and eat plants and insects.

Lizards

There are about 3,750 species of lizards in the world. They come in many shapes and sizes. Most are predators and eat everything from ants, insects, other lizards, and animals as large as goats. Their tails and legs are adapted to suit their environment. For example, if attacked at their tail, they will run and leave it behind.

Snakes

There are about 2,400 species of snakes, all varying in size from the length of your arm to that of a small car. Snakes form new scaly skin and shed their old skin as they grow, which may happen several times a year. This is called molting. Snakes have many different colors, patterns, and various ways of killing their prey.

They eat everything from ants and eggs to animals as big as goats. Their jaws can spread apart wide since they are loosely joined at the chin. Some snakes kill by using venom, injected through their sharp fangs. Other snakes wrap themselves so tightly around their prey that the animal cannot breathe and will die.

Snakes can live in water or land and have bodies adapted for survival in their environment. A sea snake has a flattened body to help push against the water. Land snakes have strong muscles to grip slippery surfaces and tree trunks and branches.

This lesson is designed to be an introduction to student-generated inquiry for first graders. For this inquiry, students generate their own questions about turtles and tortoises, lizards, or snakes since they are probably the most familiar reptiles for children this age in Delaware. By limiting the topics from which the students can choose to investigate, the teacher(s) will be better able to guide first graders through an inquiry process.

More individual and small-group attention can be provided by the teacher to students while developing questions, during data collection using a variety of resources located by the teacher, creating a visual aid and preparing a presentation to explain and share knowledge, and then by helping students begin a new inquiry process by developing a new question. Helping students learn how to collect data is an important role for the teacher(s).

Limiting the topics to three choices (turtles/tortoises, lizards, and snakes) allows the students to choose a topic of interest, while keeping the preparation of resources to be used for data collection manageable for the teacher. Teacher modeling and support will be provided for each step of the inquiry, with the goal of teaching students how to generate and choose topics independently in the future.

Learner Outcomes

By the end of the lesson the student will be able to:

- Participate as a class to generate a list of animals on the board that have the five characteristics of reptiles and then choose one to research.
- As a small group and individually, search for information about their reptile using nonfiction information books, the Internet, videos, primary and secondary sources, and their own life experiences. Share the results of their inquiry.

Learner Activities

Advance Organizer

The students are seated at their tables. The teacher asks the students if they have ever seen a reptile to activate prior knowledge. Students are given several minutes to share experiences during a group discussion.

1. The teacher tells the class that they will be watching a video called *All About Reptiles* (see Sources).
2. After the video, students participate in a class discussion about reptiles. The students generate the names of different kinds of reptiles that were in the video for the teacher to write on the whiteboard, including turtles, tortoises, lizards, and snakes.
3. The teacher circles the words "turtles," "tortoises," "lizards," and "snakes" on the board, combining the words "turtles" and "tortoises" within one circle. *"It sounds like many of you are interested in these reptiles I've circled, so let's learn more about them."*
4. The teacher asks students to choose one of these reptiles that interests them and they want to find out more about.
5. The teacher records student choices, with students divided among the three groups of reptiles: (1) turtles/tortoises, (2) lizards, and (3) snakes.
6. Students choosing the same animal will be placed in a small group together, forming three groups. At least one adult will be assigned to work with each group, including the teacher, paraprofessional, and college teacher candidate.
7. Students will meet in their separate reptile group and get out their science journals. The teacher has each student develop a question that the student wants answered about his or her reptile. Examples might be, "Where does this reptile live?" "What does my reptile eat?" "What

does my reptile look like?" "What are some different kinds of my reptile?" "Who are my reptile's predators?" Each student writes his or her question in the science journal.

8. Students are given multiple opportunities to research their reptile:

   - Students meet in small groups with their teacher, who provides a variety of trade books about the reptile for the students to read and discuss.
   - The computer teacher works with each small group, helping them find appropriate educational websites to research their reptile.
   - Students may work with parents at home to learn more about the reptile using books or discussing personal experiences.

9. The teacher provides examples on how to paraphrase information into one's own words rather than copy information directly from a book.

10. Students use the information (data) they collect to answer their question(s) about their reptile and to create a short oral presentation using a visual aid.

    For example, students could cut out pictures from a magazine or make their own illustrations to make a poster or an information book to demonstrate what they learned about their reptile. Students might visit a zoo to observe the reptile, and use photographs to create a display. Students are given time in the classroom and during art class to work in their small groups to make their visual aid and work on their presentation with teacher help.

    Students can also work on them at home with parent help, but the work must be their own. This activity requires students to paraphrase their data and present it to the class in their own words.

11. Students take turns doing their individual presentations using their visual aid in front of the class for their peers.

12. After the presentation, the student responds to questions from their peers.

Closure

- The teacher reinforces that students have learned a great deal about their reptiles to answer their original questions, citing an example of what individual students learned during the inquiry.
- The teacher asks students to think of things that they still don't know about their reptile and asks each student to pose a new question to find the answer to through further research. It is possible that students will become

interested in different reptiles researched by their peers, and they may pose a question about a new reptile, or may choose a completely new topic of interest.

Assessment

The teacher will assesses student learning of lesson outcomes during class discussions, inquiry process, and presentation. The teacher scores students using the attached rubric.

Table 7.3. Rubric for Student-Generated Inquiry of Reptiles

	0	1	2	3	4
Persistence	Never attempts activities during inquiry and presentation	Attempts but gives up quickly during inquiry and presentation	Attempts but stops at first issue during inquiry and presentation	Attempts and works through some issues during inquiry and presentation	Does not give up until all issues are resolved during inquiry and presentation
Reflection	Never uses past knowledge or experience to form new understanding	Rarely uses past knowledge or experience to form new understanding	Occasionally uses past knowledge or experience to form new understanding	Frequently uses past knowledge or experience to form new understanding	Always uses past knowledge or experience to form new understanding
Self-Direction	Refuses direction during movie, class discussion, and inquiry process	Needs constant individual attention during movie, class discussion, and inquiry process	Needs frequent reminders and direction or redirection during movie, class discussion, and inquiry process	Works with minimal direction with only occasional reminders during class activities and inquiry process	Works independently and initiates further responsibility during inquiry process
Transformation and Explanation of Data	Does not collect or explain data during presentation; does not create visual aid; does not answer questions posed by peers	Rarely explains data during presentation; visual aid lacks clear display of data; rarely answers questions	Minimally explains data during presentation; visual aid is lacking in detail; answers few questions posed by peers	Sufficiently explains data in own words during presentation; visual aid is good; answers some questions posed by peers	Fully explains data in own words during presentation; excellent visual aid; answers many questions posed by peers
Audience Participation During Class Presentations	Inattentive during all presentations; distracted; distracts other students through behaviors; does not ask questions	Inattentive during most presentations; often distracted; needs prompting to ask questions	Is an attentive listener during a few presentations; needs some prompting to ask questions	Is an attentive listener during most presentations; asks some appropriate questions	Is an attentive listener during all presentations; asking many appropriate questions.

APPENDIX D: SOCIAL INTERACTION: INTEGRATED LITERACY/ SCIENCE LITERATURE CIRCLE: PENGUINS

Content Summary for Literature Circles

Literature circles are an important way to develop both reading skills and students' ability to work with one another in a collaborative group. In literature circles, students choose their own reading materials. Small temporary groups are formed, usually comprising four or five students, based on book choice. Different groups read different books and discuss their reading with one another. Students are assigned or choose roles within the group.

The teacher acts as a facilitator, rather than as a group leader or instructor. Evaluation is through student self-evaluation and teacher observation. When students finish reading their books and sharing their reading with their classmates, new groups are formed around new reading choices.

Content Summary for Penguins

Penguins are birds and have feathers and wings, but they cannot fly. However, they have special ways of getting around. They can swim as fast as porpoises at a speed of more than fifteen miles per hour using their webbed feet and wings, which act like flippers. They can also stand upright and walk, waddling across ice by using claws on their feet to hold onto the ice. They push themselves across snow with their feet while lying on their bellies, which is called tobogganing.

Penguins spend much of their time feeding on animals, such as fish and squid, often diving down as far as one thousand feet to find squid deep in the sea. Penguins have very strong beaks that they use to defend themselves against enemies. Mother and father penguins are brave and will also use their powerful flippers as clubs to protect their nests and chicks from gulls and seals. Penguins that live in Antarctica, where the temperature goes below −76 degrees Fahrenheit, have a thick layer of blubber to keep them warm. Their sleek black and white feathers also keep them warm, even in very cold water.

There are eighteen different kinds of penguins and all of them live in the Southern Hemisphere. Many penguins live in Antarctica. Some penguins migrate from one place to another, sometimes several hundred miles, and can spend up to five months at sea. Penguins like to stay together and nest in colonies. There can be as many as one million penguins in a single colony. They find their mates in these huge crowds by recognizing each other's voices. When hunting for food in the sea, penguins also stay close together.

Breeding places are called rookeries. Penguins mate for life. They come ashore to build a nest on the ground with the materials on hand. The female lays an egg and then returns to the sea. The male hold the egg on the tops of his feet. The egg is kept warm for six weeks by a fold of skin that wraps around it like a feather blanket.

The fairy penguin is the smallest penguin in the world and is about fifteen and a half inches high. Rockhopper penguins make their nests on rocks. Royal penguins have head feathers. Adelie penguins spend most of their lives on ice and in the sea. The emperor penguin is the largest of all the penguins, growing to be three and a half feet tall and weighing over eighty-five pounds.

Today, laws in most places of the world protect penguins.

Learner Outcomes

By the end of the literature circle the student will be able to:

- Read the book independently (silently or whisper reading) and participate in a literature circle.
- Independently complete a role sheet based on reflections from the book and use it as a guide for discussion.
- Self-evaluate participation in the literature group on the recording sheet by identifying personal strengths and areas of improvement for the next literature circle.

Learner Activities

1. The students are seated on the carpet. The teacher introduces four books that will be used during the literature circles:

   - Bernard, Robin (1995). *Penguins through the year.* New York: Scholastic.
   - Gibbons, Gail (1998). *Penguins!* New York: Scholastic.
   - Jenkins, Martin (1999). *The emperor's egg.* New York: Scholastic.
   - Reed, Janet (1999). *Penguins.* New York: Scholastic.

2. Each student is given an index card to write down his or her first, second, and third book choice. Students will be encouraged to choose a book that matches their interests and reading level the closest.
3. The teacher looks over the index cards and forms four literature circles, each containing four to six students.
4. The teacher passes out role sheets to each group (six types) and explains them. Each student chooses a different role to complete.

5. Multiple copies of the same book are given to students in each group. The students independently read the book assigned to their group.
6. Beginning readers at this age level may require extra reading support to comprehend text. The teacher may act as a facilitator for the group to pair up students for buddy reading, echo reading with a partner, or group choral reading. The book can also be recorded on tape for a nonreader to listen to, if necessary.
7. Students write a reflection on their own role sheet.
8. Students are given a recording sheet to write four facts they learned about penguins.
9. Students meet in their literature circle to discuss their book using their role sheets and recording sheets with four facts about penguins as a guide. The discussion is extended beyond the information on the sheets.
10. Each circle group briefly summarizes their book for the class. The group also shares their opinions of the book. Each member of the group shares at least one fact that he or she learned about penguins.

Closure

- Students are introduced to other books about penguins found in the classroom library that they can read on their own.
- Each student is given a self-evaluation form to complete. It includes a rubric on the front and sentence completion on the back. This information will be used to help both the teacher and students plan for the next literature circle. New literature groups will be formed around new reading choices.

Assessment

Observe students and keep anecdotal records. Collect role sheets, recording sheets, and self-evaluation sheets to score rubrics and use this information to form new literature circles in the future.

Self-Evaluation for Literature Circle

Use the key to self-evaluate your participation in literature circle activities.

1 = Didn't do it at all or   2 = Did it okay   3 = Did it great!
had a lot of trouble
doing it

1. I filled out my role sheet.	1	2	3

2. The information on my role sheet showed that I carefully read and understood the book.	1	2	3
3. I shared the information on my role sheet with the people in my group when we discussed the book.	1	2	3
4. I listened carefully when other people shared their information in our group.	1	2	3
5. I wrote down four facts that I learned about penguins.	1	2	3
6. I helped summarize the book and give a group opinion on it for my whole class.	1	2	3

Set goals for yourself for the next literature circle by completing the following sentences:

My favorite part about this literature circle was . . .

To improve my participation in the next literature circle, I will . . .

Next time, I would like to read a book about . . .

Because . . .

Fact Finder: Role Sheets

Book Title:

Directions: Write down five facts that you learned about penguins from this book that you can share with your literature circle group.

1.

2.

3.

4.

5.

Chef

Book Title:

Find "spicy" descriptive words that the author used to make this book interesting. Record the words and page numbers. Be prepared to talk about the spicy words with your group. You can use the back of the paper if necessary.

1.   page

2.   page

3.   page

4.   page

5.   page

6.   page

Illustrator

Book Title:

Draw a picture of a penguin. Draw the habitat where the penguin lives as a background. Be prepared to talk about your picture and tell what kind of penguin you drew.

Question Maniac

Book Title:

After reading your book, write down questions that you still have about penguins. Be prepared to talk about how you can find out answers to your questions.

1.

2.

3.

4.

5.

Geography Expert

Book Title:

Where in the world do penguins live? Draw a map and label it to show where different kinds of penguins live on Earth. Be prepared to talk about your map.

Bird Watcher

Book Title:

Penguins are a kind of bird. Write down the names of as many different kinds of birds besides penguins that you know. Be prepared to talk about what you know about the birds!

1.
2.
3.
4.
5.
6.
7.
8.
9.
10.
11.
12.
13.
14.

Table 7.4. Rubric for Literature Circles

	0	1	2	3	4
Persistence	Never attempts activities during literature-circle activities	Attempts but gives up quickly during literature-circle activities	Attempts but stops at first issue during literature-circle activities	Attempts and works through some issues during literature-circle activities	Does not give up until all issues are resolved during literature-circle activities
Reflection	Never uses past knowledge or experience to form new understanding	Rarely uses past knowledge or experience to form new understanding	Occasionally uses past knowledge or experience to form new understanding	Frequently uses past knowledge or experience to form new understanding	Always uses past knowledge or experience to form new understanding
Self-Direction	Refuses direction during literature-circle activities	Needs constant individual attention during literature-circle activities	Needs frequent reminders and direction or redirection during literature-circle activities	Works with minimal direction with only occasional reminders during literature-circle activities	Works independently and initiates further responsibility during literature-circle activities
Content Knowledge about Penguins	Does not complete role sheet; does not orally share information; is not an attentive listener during literature-circle activities; does not self-evaluate	Rarely completes role sheet; rarely orally shares information; rarely listens attentively during literature-circle activities; little, if any, self-evaluation	Minimally completes role sheet; minimally orally shares information; listens attentively during literature-circle activities some of the time; self-evaluates only minimally	Sufficiently completes role sheet; orally shares information sufficiently; usually listens attentively during literature-circle activities; self-evaluates well using reflection	Fully completes role sheet; fully orally shares information and is an attentive listener during literature-circle activities; self-evaluates fully, reflectively, and thoughtfully

Teaching Memoir: The Leader or the Boss?

Heidi L. Greene

Even before the 8:00 bell rings, "lead management" is in effect. Like most mornings, this one is spent in the cafeteria, mingling with the students, building relationships. I congratulate Erik on the athletic award he won last night, inquire about Kim's senior thesis topic, compliment Nikki on her outfit, ask Natalie if she can meet with me after school to discuss the talent show she is planning, and let Zack know that I notice that he has been on time the last three days.

These thirty-second interactions help me get a pulse for the students and where they are emotionally that day, not to mention help reinforce to students that I care about their success. As the administrator of a school dedicated to a constructivist philosophy of learning, I know the importance that relationships play in the success of our school. William Glasser, in his writings about Choice Theory, discusses the difference between lead management and boss management. From the beginning of my administrative career, I had determined to be a leader in my school, not the boss.

As the morning gets into full swing, Mrs. Whittingham shows up at my door, wanting to discuss a concern she has with Mr. Lane, who teaches across the hall from her. She explains that she is often interrupted by unruly behavior and loud voices from the other classroom. Her strategy so far has been to shut her door, complain to some of her colleagues, and avoid the teacher.

As Mrs. Whittingham starts to talk, I sit back and listen, acknowledging her frustration. At this point I have several options. I can speak to Mr. Lane about the concerns, I can ignore them and hope they will just improve on their own, or I can guide Mrs. Whittingham in the process of addressing her own concerns.

When she is finished talking, I ask, "Are you telling me this because you want my help or because you need to vent?"

Mrs. Whittingham admits to wanting both. We spend some time talking about our school's goal of having a collegial environment, one where staff can have constructive conversations with one another.

I ask, "If another teacher came to me with a concern about you, what advice would you want me to give her?"

Mrs. Whittingham quickly says, "Well, I hope you would ask her if she has shared her concern with me, and if she had not, then you would encourage her to talk to me."

I have to say very little more because Mrs. Whittingham has really solved her own problem. She agrees to talk to Mr. Lane and let him know that the noise coming from his room is distracting to her students.

After lunch, I head down to the science room for my previously scheduled meeting with Mrs. Monroe, a new teacher in our school. I have been in her room several times during the last month, and it is clear that she has several classroom-management issues. My intention today is to discuss these concerns with her and figure out what support she needs.

I start off by giving Mrs. Monroe the opportunity to reflect on her practices before I share my own observations. I say, "When I stopped by yesterday, you were teaching a lesson on the water cycle. How do you think class went yesterday? What was successful and what would you change?"

She immediately starts talking about the students who were talking while she was talking.

I ask, "How did you handle that?"

She thinks for a moment and says, "I just kept on talking because I didn't know what else to do. They just refuse to pay attention."

I ask Mrs. Monroe to tell me what she wants her classroom to be like. We spend the rest of our time brainstorming ways to get to that vision. My goal is to get her to think of changes she can make, rather than trying to change the kids. She agrees to try a few of the strategies and I commit to checking in with her progress later next week.

In the hall before the last class of the day, I see Dan walking away from Mrs. Carr, who is clearly trying to talk to him. As Dan gets closer to me, I say, "What are you doing?"

He answers, "Man, Mrs. Carr is always on my case. She's trying to take my headphones away, and now I'm going to be late to class."

I reply, "So if a teacher is trying to talk to you, what is the responsible thing to do?"

He answers, "Listen to what she has to say, I guess."

"OK," I say, "So what do you need to do?" Dan heads back to Mrs. Carr.

The day is winding down. I'm off to bus duty, yet another chance to strengthen relationships with teachers, parents, and students.

REFERENCE

Glasser, W. (1998). *Choice theory: A new psychology of personal freedom.* New York: Harper-Collins.

Chapter Eight

Teaching Study: A New Definition of Professional Development

Laura M. Leach

When educators in the United States hear the words "professional development," they typically think of workshops in the areas of content, pedagogy, counseling, and more. A shift occurred when the TIMSS (Third International Math and Science Study) compared the performance of students in Japan, the United States, and Germany, and as a result, an interest in Japanese lesson study grew as a way to improve professional development in the United States.

This chapter describes Japanese lesson study and discusses how this experience goes beyond the typical definition of professional development in the United States. Also included is an account of how teachers at a small charter school in Delaware evolved as they participated in a process adapted from the principles and practices of Japanese lesson study.

This chapter is especially appropriate as the last chapter of a book on constructivist classroom practices. It provides a structure through which we, as teachers, can look at our practice through a constructivist lens. How do we *know* our students are learning? What else can we do to increase student learning? And, how can the tenets of Japanese lesson study help us make these determinations and put them into practice?

WHAT IS JAPANESE LESSON/TEACHING STUDY?

Many researchers interested in Japanese lesson study attribute its growing popularity to Stigler and Hiebert's (1999) book *The Teaching Gap: Best Ideas from the World's Teachers for Improving Education in the Classroom.*

131

Japanese lesson study, which has also been translated as "teaching study," is a practice in which teams of teachers meet throughout the year to work collaboratively on the design and implementation of lessons to be taught to their own students.

Makoto Yoshida (Fernandez & Yoshida, 2004) actually coined the phrase "lesson study," which he translated from the Japanese term *"jugyou ken-kyuu."* This translation points to the interpretation that lesson study serves the purpose of collecting and documenting sets of perfected lessons. However, the term *"jugyou"* in Japanese can also mean "teaching" and this leads to a more relevant interpretation of the experience with the focus not on something as limiting as a lesson, but on the whole of teaching. For this reason, the process described in this chapter will be referred to as "teaching study."

The process of teaching study is intensive and involves six steps (Fernandez & Yoshida, 2004):

1. Teams of teachers (usually teaching the same grade level or the same content area) plan a lesson together. They determine the concept to be taught; set learner outcomes, activities, and assessments; gather materials; and predict possible student responses to the lesson.
2. One team member teaches the lesson to his or her students as the other members do a live observation, taking field notes.
3. The team meets to discuss the lesson and reflect on feedback from the live observations.
4. The team revises the lesson making any necessary changes (Fernandez and Yoshida actually say this step could be optional because some groups will want to continue with the original lesson to learn more about it before revision takes place).
5. Another team member teaches the same lesson (or the new version if one was created). This continues with a different member from the team until all have taught the lesson and received feedback from the members who are observing.
6. The team members share final reflections and use their new knowledge to inform the planning of future lessons and units.

Important to this process is a shared long-term goal that the teachers have decided upon before the teaching study begins. Examples of learning goals might be enabling students to become critical thinkers or self-directed learners. Content-specific goals include providing activities that help students to *become* "historians" or "scientists" or "writers" rather than simply students who study and take a test on the current science unit or write to a prompt.

Throughout the implementation and observations, focus is on the aspects of the lesson (concepts, students' discourse, outcomes, etc.) and is *not* focused solely on the teacher. Although this is contrary to typical classroom evaluation, it is a crucial part of the teaching study process. The process provides a framework in which the teachers' knowledge is transformed into meaningful instruction for students (Hiebert, Gallimore, & Stigler, 2002), which often does not happen when teachers only receive evaluation of their teaching skills.

GOING BEYOND PROFESSIONAL DEVELOPMENT

Teaching study is not a "strategy" that need only be implemented to improve teaching. Rather, it is a recursive, joint practice from which could evolve many different experiences.

Ask any educator in the United States what they do during professional development provided by their district during teacher in-service days (which would be different from professional development provided by national organizations or conferences that teachers attend outside of their school). They may say that they learn strategies to give tests to monitor reading levels, familiarize themselves with a set of new textbooks adopted by their district, or find out about new state initiatives.

These responses are shared by teachers across the country and are often followed by groans that show annoyance with what has come to be known as professional development. Take it a step further and ask teachers if they believe the professional development they have received has actually helped them to develop and grow as professionals or if it has helped their students learn. The answer is often a resounding "no."

Of course, not all professional development provided by districts is as grim. Some schools provide teachers with more meaningful experiences and view professional development as something more than what was described in the above paragraphs. For example, the professional development provided at a small charter school in Delaware is unique and effective.

As part of the charter, which espouses the constructivist paradigm, teachers at the school are required to write their own curriculum. There are no textbooks used at the schools, and thus teachers work in collaborative teams by grade levels to study the national and state standards, create concept maps and content summaries, develop focus questions, write outcomes and assessments, and develop learning activities. Writing curriculum is an important endeavor. Professional development is typically focused on developing and discussing curriculum.

The teachers at the charter school work closely on grade-level or content-specific teams. In teaching study, "membership" on a team is not the only goal, but rather forming professional communities that study their teaching through a continuous and recursive process.

Teaching can be seen as a cultural activity. Many of the books written about Japanese lesson study refer to the need for teachers to view teaching as a cultural endeavor that involves educators, students, and families working within a community. Like any community, this group of people has particular behavior patterns, beliefs, and expectations that sometimes become prohibitive to important change. Teaching study allows participants to view their teaching through this cultural lens and think about their roles in a different way. This can result in positive changes in attitudes, beliefs, behaviors, and discourse.

In the United States, teaching is typically thought of as having separate parts (like content, pedagogy, assessments, activities, etc.). Thus, American educators tend to think of curriculum as a collection of materials, a book, or a text that is often handed to them from the district level. Rarely are these educators given the opportunity to discuss the complexity of curriculum or to develop curriculum for their students. And yet constructivist teaching demands just that. Teaching study encourages discussion around how curriculum fits into students' learning rather than how to fit isolated pieces of curriculum into students' heads.

THE PILOT STUDY

The teaching study at the charter school was first done as a pilot study, focusing on a team of fourth- and fifth-grade teachers who had volunteered to begin the process. The research question that was asked was, *Would teaching study precipitate any change in the culture among the team of teachers, specifically relating to their discussion with each other regarding the curriculum in their classrooms?*

The teachers began the process by discussing characteristics that they ideally would like to see in their students, such as reflective thinking and intrinsic motivation to learn. Then they decided on their long-term goal: to encourage students to use reflective thinking to evaluate their learning process in order to develop intrinsic motivation. The teaching study would take place during a reader's workshop in each teacher's classroom.

After developing their long-term goal, they came up with content goals based on the reader's workshop curriculum they had previously established. Their content goals were to develop:

• Critical readers who understand, identify, and express components of quality literature.
• Critical readers who understand and utilize metacognitive strategies.

The team then created process goals based on their teaching study. The process goals for students were the following:

- To participate in read-aloud discussions by sharing metacognitive strategies and components of quality literature.
- To construct deeper meaning from literature through participation in reader's workshop.
- To read for a variety of purposes across genres.
- To communicate in a variety of ways.

Once their content and process goals were developed, the teachers began discussing lesson goals for the live observations that would be done. Their lesson goal was the following:

- Students will reflect on growth as an individual through their participation in reader's workshop.

This goal would be monitored through individual semi-structured student interviews during the conferences held during reader's workshop. As the teachers discussed their goals, they talked about curriculum and how it is a formative experience not only for the students, but also for the teachers. They looked forward to the live observations.

Once the team established the goals for teaching study, they began by observing one teacher's classroom. The teachers took notes and talked to students as they observed. The teaching study team met after the lesson to discuss observations.

The teachers talked about how they were able to see a different view through observing and were able to focus more on student questions and ideas more as the observer rather than the teacher. The teachers discussed the fact that they could hear more conversations between the students as the observers. They discussed how this role enabled them to view curriculum as a formative course or path rather than a lesson that met the stated objectives. The teachers reflected on the fact that the students were forming new ideas and changing as readers through their participation in reader's workshop.

The teaching study continued until the teachers had observed in all four classrooms. Since their content, process, and lesson goals were broad, it allowed the teachers to focus on how the students were truly viewing the process of reader's workshop and what they were gaining from it. All of the teachers discussed how powerful the live observations were. They each said that it was a great learning experience to be able to watch the other classes and teachers in action. The teachers also agreed that the meetings after the observations allowed for discussion that may not have typically occurred without the practice of teaching study.

The teachers recognized the observations as a potent learning experience that reinforced the idea that teaching study was truly a form of professional development. When asked if the teachers viewed this process as an experience that led to professional growth, they answered "yes" without hesitation. The teachers were excited to continue the observations and the teaching study practice. They did state that it took time away from their own classrooms, and that the support of the school administrators was key, but they each viewed the time as extremely valuable.

Was the research question answered? Would teaching study precipitate a change in the culture among the team of teachers? The short answer is yes. The teachers discovered that trust was perhaps the most important aspect of the teaching study. As that trust developed, the discourse changed from being focused on teacher actions to discussion of student discourse, ideas, and learning. Building trust in the school was crucial, and that trust evolved through the joint practice of teaching study.

CONCLUSION

The teachers viewed teaching study as a very powerful practice that led to insight into their teaching and into the formative growth of their students and themselves. It allowed them to view curriculum as an experience in which they played a major role, rather than a checklist of content to cover.

Another team of teachers was eager to participate in the teaching study. The discourse among the teams changed as teachers began discussing the complexity of curriculum rather than simply planning for the week. Teaching study helped the teachers to focus on important aspects of school such as curriculum development, constructivist teaching, student learning, and creating a school culture of trust and growth and a passion for teaching and learning.

As teaching study continues at the school, teachers will grow as professionals and gain a focused insight into their students' learning. The observations will allow for the culture of teaching at the school to be passed on to other teachers. The discourse will continue to show evidence of the culture of the school.

Teaching study is powerful professional development. It encourages educators to bring out their curriculum and their teaching practices from behind closed doors. They can form teaching teams and create the learning communities that help define a school's culture. Teaching study provides the opportunity to share that culture and determine best practices together.

REFERENCES

Fernandez, C., & Yoshida, M. (2004). *Lesson study: A Japanese approach to improving mathematics teaching and learning.* Mahwah, NJ: Lawrence Erlbaum.

Hiebert, J., Gallimore, R., & Stigler, J. (2002). A knowledge base for the teaching profession: What would it look like and how can we get one? *Educational Researcher, 31*(5), 3–15.

Stigler, J., & Hiebert, J. (1999). *The teaching gap: Best ideas from the world's teachers for improving education in the classroom.* New York: Free Press.

Epilogue

This book has showcased constructivist practices that teach content the way students learn. The authors have shared their passions for teaching and the teaching strategies that have worked for them and their students. The hope is that you have gained some new insights, some new beliefs, some new concepts that will affect your practice and your students.

The final teaching memoir is yours. What are your successes? What challenges have you overcome? What problems still bother you? What can you share with other teachers? What have your students taught you? What is *your* story? What do you *want* it to be?

Your story is important. Your impact is important. Begin now. Walk across the hall and share your experience with literature circles or Three-Point Book Club with a colleague. Gather your grade-level team and work together on planning a teaching study. Invite your principal into your classroom to read with your students. Take your students on a walk to collect specimens for their nature journals. Plan a debate between two classes. Read more about the philosophy of constructivism and reflect on how you and your students learn.

We, the authors of this book, wish you a teaching memoir filled with challenge and triumph, discovery and learning, tears and laughter, and most important, joy in the journey.

Contributors

Jill E. Cole, EdD, is associate professor of education at Wesley College and serves as the program chair for education K–8. She previously taught elementary and middle school for twenty-four years.

Thomas B. Cole is retired from Caterpillar, Inc., where he was a senior systems analyst in information technology.

Kathleen M. Doyle, MA, is currently a social studies teacher at Campus Community High School in her twenty-fifth year of teaching. She has also taught a graduate-level course for teachers and mentored many others.

Heidi L. Greene, MS in education, is the building administrator for Campus Community High School. She previously taught middle school language arts.

Charmaine M. Herrera, MA, MEd, teaches sixth- and seventh-grade language arts at Campus Community School and is currently a doctoral candidate at the University of Delaware.

Marcia P. Lawton, PhD, is professor of education at Wesley College. Previously, she taught special education for ten years, literacy methods and special education courses for Delaware State University and the University of Delaware, and worked with teachers to develop clinical methods for Title I reading programs.

Laura M. Leach, MEd, teaches a second- and third-grade multiage classroom at Campus Community School. She is a doctoral candidate at the University of Delaware.

Patti L. Sandy, MEd, has been a teacher for thirty-three years. She is a National Board Certified Teacher at Campus Community School, where she teaches first grade.

Robin D. Smith, MBA, is a business educator at Campus Community High School. Previously, she worked in the Advancement Offices of Wesley College, at Wilmington Friends School, and for Progressive Insurance.

Arielle Suggs is a teacher candidate in her junior year at Wesley College.

D. Colette Wheatley, MEd, is an instructor of education and field placement coordinator at Wesley College. Previously, she taught in a fifth-grade classroom for thirty-one years.

Jamie Whitman-Smithe, PhD, is associate professor of education at Wesley College. Previously, she taught middle school and in a school for persons with disabilities.

CPSIA information can be obtained at www.ICGtesting.com
Printed in the USA
BVOW011221110112

280246BV00001B/6/P